Family Talk

May God bless & Strengthen
you and your family

Jim Priest

by Jim Priest

This material is the copyrighted work of the author and first appeared as columns in The Daily Oklahoman, a copyrighted publication of the Oklahoma Publishing Company, whose cooperation is gratefully acknowledged. (© 1998 The Oklahoma Publishing Company)

Printed in the United States of America
Oklahoma City, Oklahoma
ISBN #1-885473-98-2

Produced by:

Pre-Production Press
2717 NW 50th
Oklahoma City, OK 73112
(405) 946-0621

Pre-Production Press is an imprint of
Wood 'N' Barnes Publishing & Distribution

To order copies of this book, please call:
Jean Barnes Books
2717 NW 50th
OKC, OK 73112
405-946-0621 • 800-678-0621

Acknowledgments

Deep gratitude and high honor are owed
and gladly given to:

- My sovereign God, who came up with the idea of marriage and family. We're sorry we've messed things up and we hope you'll help us put things aright.

- Marge & Ted Priest, my faithful and loving parents, who taught me what marriage and family is all about in the real world and served as role models and mentors.

- My love, my partner, my proofreader, my wife Diane who made me the luckiest guy on earth twenty years ago.

- My daughter Amanda, the beloved one, who never fails to energize and encourage me, and who lights up my life with her smile.

- My only begotten son, Spence, in whom I am well pleased. He gives me hope for the future of Godly men.

- The folks at the Daily Oklahoman who graciously provide me the opportunity to encourage people to be faithful to their marriage and family commitments.

- Mony Cunningham, my long time friend, who assured me I had written something worth reading and shepherded me through the publication process.

Deo gratias

About the Author

Jim Priest is a husband of one, father of two, trial attorney, newspaper columnist, seminar speaker and Sunday School teacher. Raised in upstate New York, he graduated from Houghton College and Syracuse University Law School, married a Texas girl, and moved to Oklahoma City, Oklahoma in 1980.

Jim's life mission statement reads:

> *"My life purpose is to encourage my family, friends and others in my sphere of influence to live lives of commitment to their families, and to God and His Word, by living a Godly life, applying God's word to every situation I face, and teaching others to do so. I am especially dedicated to encouraging men to be faithful to their God, their marriage vows and their family responsibility."*

Jim is available as a conference or seminar speaker on the topics of family, ethics, law and Christian living.

Jim may be contacted at:
6109 Gun Hill Way
Oklahoma City, OK 73132
405-722-6890
email: jpriest1@juno.com

Introduction

In October 1996, I began writing a weekly column for Oklahoma City's daily newspaper, The Daily Oklahoman. The column was the fruition of an idea I'd had for several years. I wanted to remind my community about the critical importance of marriage and family. Divorce rates were discouragingly high (they still are) and families were being pulled in all directions (they still are). Rather than writing another book, I decided I'd try a different medium: the newspaper.

I figured some folks who might not read a book on marriage or family would be willing to read a short newspaper column. So the idea of Family Talk was born and became a reality with the encouragement of Oklahoma Publishing Company President, Ed Martin and Community editor, Linda Lynn.

So why this book? People who read the column encouraged me to compile the articles in some way. Many folks told me they file away the columns and plan to read them or use them in the future. Other people said they clip the articles and mail them to a friend or relative in another state; they wanted to have a collection to send. In response to these readers' urgings, I undertook this project and it is my sincere hope and prayer it will be helpful to your marriage and family, now or in the future.

I'm a pragmatist by personality and training. I know one book among hundreds of thousands published will not make a world shattering difference. But I'm like the guy who walked along a sandy shore early one morning trying to save starfish who had washed up on the beach during the night. He would pick them up and hurl them back into the ocean, one by one. After flinging starfish for some time the man was approached by a pessimistic observer who said, "There are thousands of starfish dying up and down the beach. You can't possibly hope to make a difference!" The fish-flinger picked up another starfish, threw it into the surf and replied, "I guess you're right, but at least I made a difference for that one."

If I can make a positive difference in your marriage or family, this book will have been worth the effort.

Contents

≈ family talk

Character

family talk

Being a Person of Integrity

Danny was one of the most likable men I ever knew. I met Danny when I first moved to Oklahoma City in 1980. He was a quick smiling, genuinely friendly guy who made my wife and me feel welcome in a new city. Danny and his wife were very successful folks both professionally and personally: two wonderful children, lots of friends and a thriving paint contracting business. Thriving at least until the oil bust hit Oklahoma. The paint contracting business—and a lot of other businesses—went belly up, and it didn't leave Danny unscathed either. But through it all Danny and his wife remained faithful members of my Sunday School class and our church—still smiling, still friendly.

One night in the Wednesday evening service, Danny stood to his feet and with great emotion in his voice confessed to something he said he wasn't very proud of. It seems Danny and his two children, Lana and Kent, were driving down 39th Street to their home when they saw several rolls of sod lying by the side of the road. Danny could see it was good sod—the kind they lay on golf greens—the kind neighbors envy when it's on your lawn. Apparently the rolls had fallen off a sod truck and the truck was now long gone. Danny quickly pulled over. He had just the spot for that sod—a bare spot in his lawn that had defied lawn seed for months. Danny figured this sod was just the thing for that stubborn spot of earth. He threw it in the back of his pick-up and headed down the road with it. After about 10 miles they overtook a sod truck pulled over to the side of the road, the driver wrestling valiantly with the remaining sod, trying to re-secure the load. In a flash the "rest of the story" became evident. The sod Danny picked up belonged on that truck. But Danny kept driving. As they sped by, his son said "Daddy, do you think that's the truck that lost the sod we found?" Danny drove on in silence, suppressing the twinge of guilt he felt.

Danny planted that grass in that bare spot the same night. It fit just right. He watered it, cared for it and mowed it. Every time he went near it, he felt that gnawing guilt until it just ate at him so long he had to confess it to someone. So Danny confessed it to God and asked for forgiveness. He also told his sister and admitted that even after asking forgiveness he still didn't feel right about it. "What should I do?" he asked. "Dig it up," his sister told him. "Dig it up, and take your children and wife out there to show them what you did and confess it to them; ask them to forgive you too. Then place rocks over that spot like they did in the Old Testament to remember a significant event. And don't ever compromise your integrity again."

So Danny did what his sister advised. And the rocks served as a reminder to him to maintain his integrity with passion and zeal, even in the smallest events of life.

You may think Danny is a little strange—getting worked up over a little sod that didn't mean that much to anyone. I think he's a little strange, but in a good way—different than most of the rest of the world. Do you think Danny will lightly compromise his integrity in anything, large or small, again? Do you think his wife will, or his daughter or his son? Or, do you think Danny's family will remember that lesson for the rest of their lives? I know I will, and it serves as an inspiration to me to reject little compromises in my integrity. It reminds me that integrity begins in the home, and it includes even the seemingly small things in our lives. Decide now to be a person of integrity in your home, and rather than just talking to your kids about making wise and moral choices, live it out in front of them.

✧ ✧ ✧

2

More is Caught than Taught

Saint Francis of Assisi, the respected founder of the Franciscan order, once invited a young monk to accompany him to preach in town. The devout novice jumped at the opportunity, and they both headed off toward the village. The rookie envisioned great crowds of people enthralled by Saint Francis' sermons and many heathens' lives being changed. As they entered the city the two headed off the main road and spent most of the morning chatting with shopkeepers, peddlers and average citizens. A kind word, a helpful hand and a smile were given to each. After spending most of the day in this kind of activity, Saint Francis turned to head back to the abbey.

"Father, have you forgotten we came to town to preach?" asked the young man.

"My son, we *have* preached," replied Saint Francis. "We have been seen by many. Our behavior has been closely watched and our attitudes measured. Our words have been overheard. It was by this that we preached our morning sermon."

If we are to truly impact our children with principles of integrity and moral values, we must begin with this lesson of Saint Francis. More is caught than taught. We have to walk the talk. Parents must practice what they preach. If the younger generation seems to lack civility, morality or integrity, perhaps it is because the older generation has failed to adequately model it. It is not enough to simply instruct children to do right—they must see us live it out in our daily lives.

The Old Testament book of Deuteronomy puts it this way: "And these words (the commandments of God) shall be on your heart and you shall teach them diligently to your children and shall talk of them when you sit in your house and when you walk by the way and when you lie down and when you rise up" (Deuteronomy 6:6-7). From this ancient command we notice several things about raising an ethical generation.

We must take morality to heart. Without internalizing our ethics and practicing those principles every day, all our talk about being "good people" and making "right decisions" will fall on the deaf ears of our children. Young people won't listen to a dad who scolds them for cheating in school but smiles slyly as he cheats on his tax return. A mom cannot speak convincingly to a daughter about truth-telling if she engages in little white lies on a daily basis. Our kids have a built in "bull" detector, and the lights flash and the alarm goes off whenever our talk doesn't match our walk. The commandments of moral conduct must be "on our heart."

We must diligently teach morality. Diligence requires constant attention. This means every day, every hour, every moment. There can be no vacations from integrity. Diligence in teaching moral principles does not mean we, as parents, will lead perfect lives. But it does mean that when we make a bad choice or stub our ethical toe, we'll readily admit it and get back on the path. Diligence is a sister to

persistence and a kissing cousin of consistency. As tiresome
as it may seem, we must be diligent in living morally and
instructing our children to follow our lead. They must know,
without doubt, that there is right and wrong. There is a
"true north" on the ethical map, and our decisions must be
directed by that moral compass or we'll be lost.

We must teach morality in the everyday moments of life. Notice this Old Testament passage doesn't address formal class-
room teaching about the commandments. It doesn't legis-
late a curriculum to be taught in school or a rigid instruction manual to be zealously followed. Instead we are commanded to teach when we are just "hanging out" with our
kids—sitting, walking, late at night, early in the morning—
wherever we find an opportunity to make a point or draw
an analogy. Look for casual opportunities to teach your
children moral and ethical conduct by noting good examples
or pointing out bad ones. Discuss the "morality" (or lack of
it) in television programs you watch together. Talk about
the ethics of decisions you see being made. Sometimes we're
reluctant to be "judgmental", but we cannot let this reluctance override our obligation to instruct our children about
good and evil. The world has plenty of both to comment
upon. Seize those teachable moments with your children.

Saint Francis would have agreed with the person who said
"Who you are speaks so loudly I can't hear what you're saying." Be careful that your saying and your doing are consistent. Make sure you place the commandments on your
own heart and then diligently teach them to your children
as you walk down the road of life. ✢

3

Teach and Live a Life of Discipline

No doubt about it, the world belongs to the disciplined. Call it what you will—hustle, perseverance, tenacity, staying power—it all boils down to one thing: discipline. It's the thing that makes you do *what* you should do, *when* you should do it, in the *way* you should do it, whether or not you *want* to do it. It amounts to acting better than you feel. I believe it's discipline we need in our own lives, and it's discipline we need to teach in our families.

I've become convinced that only a few people are naturally disciplined. The reason for this is most of us are emotional creatures. We do things because we "feel like it." Wouldn't most of us prefer to avoid responsibility rather than embrace it? Aren't we often tempted to sit and watch TV when we should be mowing the grass? Don't we find a million excuses to put off writing a friend or helping the widow down the street with her plumbing problems? Come on, admit it. Secretly, you're a discipline drop-out. You give in to your emotions. You like to act the way you feel. And when we live undisciplined lives, we model behavior our family members observe and follow—especially our children.

By natural disposition, I'm not very disciplined. I'd rather chuck my tools in a heap on the work bench than put them in their proper place (Sorry about that, Dad). I'd rather not make my bed every morning (Sorry about that, Mom). But

I've learned that even we undisciplined types can become disciplined. We can see things through to completion, do them thoroughly and do them well.

The key to being disciplined is part motivation, part planning and part staying power. Mostly, it's just doing what needs to be done, regardless of how you feel. The sooner we begin living and modeling discipline in our homes, the sooner our families and our country will get back on the right track.

How do we begin to model and teach discipline in our homes?

Recognize yourself for what you are. You're not very disciplined by nature. That's ok. You can make yourself more disciplined. Recognize that your emotions are not your control center—your mind is. You can direct yourself to do the thing that ought to be done, regardless of whether you want to do it. If we model this behavior in our homes, our family members are more likely to pick up the discipline habit.

Begin with the small things. Discipline yourself and your family members to make your beds every day shortly after awakening. Force yourself to go to bed instead of waiting for the test pattern screen to appear on the TV. Keep your personal appearance neat and clean, clothes pressed, shoes shined, fingernails clipped and hair combed. Does this sound a little too basic? Maybe so. But if you're not doing these basic things, the higher levels of discipline will continue to elude you.

Just keep going. Don't get discouraged and quit when you break your resolution, or when you start smoking again, or when you lapse back into undiscipline. The difference between a successful person and an unsuccessful one is perseverance. The Old Testament wisdom in Proverbs 24:16 says "A righteous man falls down seven times and yet gets up." It's not that the righteous person never falls, he or she just gets up and keeps going. You can do the same.

Surround yourself with people who are also trying to be disciplined. I'm not talking about only associating with compulsive folks who eat no-fat food, jog 10 miles daily, have neat garages and cupboards and look like they press their underwear. I'm talking about becoming pals with a fellow struggler who is doing his or her best to become a disciplined person one day and one inch at a time. We become like those with whom we associate—so hang out with folks who are bringing themselves in line. As you acquire the habit of discipline, your family members will be watching and learning.

Finally, don't forget the reward. Believe me, hard work is most definitely not its own reward. Whatever your task, set intermediate goals that will move you toward accomplishment and then provide some little reward when the intermediate goals are reached. This maintains motivation and keeps you on the discipline track.

If we model discipline in our lives and teach it in our homes, we'll be building a stronger tomorrow for our family and our nation. One habit at a time. One family at a time.

✢ ✢ ✢

4

TDD
A New Deadly Disease

Most of us have heard of ADD—Attention Deficit Disorder. It's a problem that has emerged in recent years as the subject of much diagnosis, debate and prescription medicine. But I'm convinced that ADD does not compare with another new malady that has become epidemic: TDD—Tact Deficit Disorder.

Tact Deficit Disorder is a severely low allocation of one of humanity's most needed elements—tact. You know what tact is. It's the discipline that makes you bite your tongue when you want to lash someone with it. It's the ability to engage your mind before putting your mouth in gear. It's the healthy dose of concern for others that tempers our otherwise selfish actions. In short, tact is thinking about and putting others first instead of doing or saying whatever you please.

As a lawyer I've seen the astonishing spread of TDD throughout corporate America. In fact, most of the lawsuits I'm involved in could have been avoided if the participants had not been afflicted by TDD. The same thing is true in the family. Marital discord, parent-child fights and sibling rivalry could all be reduced or eliminated if TDD could be brought under control. I can only imagine how many divorces could be avoided if this dreaded disease could be cured.

Of course TDD is not a recent phenomena. The Old Testament tells of many Bible characters who suffered from the ailment. People like the friends of Job who came to console him after the death of his sons and daughters by telling him he had probably sinned and deserved the punishment. Even a Bible hero like the multi-color-coated Joseph had a touch of TDD when he told his father and brothers he had a dream about them bowing down and worshipping him. We can think of a lot of current day folks who are more recent victims of this illness: Dennis Rodman, Jerry Springer, Howard Stern. The list could go on and on.

TDD is, unfortunately, terribly contagious. One person infected with it can swiftly spread it to others with deadly results. How it got started is unknown, and its treatment is uncertain. One thing that is known for sure is TDD can be cured. But the cure is a "home remedy."

To eliminate TDD we must begin in our homes to teach and display tact. Knocking before you enter a bedroom. Serving another family member first at the supper table. Saying please and thank you and "yes ma'am" and "no sir." I'm not talking about just teaching your kids to do these things; I'm talking about modeling them as parents.

I have a wonderful and peculiar memory of my father. Anytime we would leave the house together early in the morning—before anyone else in our house or our neighbor's house was awake, Pa would go through an odd ritual with his car. We would sneak quietly out the front door, easing the storm and glass doors shut like stealthy burglars. Then we would go to the old Impala in the driveway and open the doors to get in. But wait! "Don't slam that door shut,"

Pa would remind me. "It might wake the neighbors." So we would just "click" the door shut until we were out of the driveway and down the street. At the first stop sign we'd open and shut our doors properly and safely. All that effort just so we wouldn't wake the neighbors or our other family members in the early morning hours with the slam of a car door.

When you think about it, maybe Pa's little ritual didn't make all that much sense. Starting the car engine was probably noisy enough all by itself to wake the neighbors. And banging our door shut down the street had the potential of waking those folks whose house was located by the stop sign. But whether his exercise in tact made sense or not I'll always remember the underlying lesson: show concern for others by the way you act.

My parents taught me that same lesson about my words. As a child you probably heard the same well worn phrase I heard throughout my growing up years "If you can't say something nice about someone, don't say anything at all." With some people, sometimes the kindest thing I could do was to keep my mouth shut. But whichever person was the subject of discussion around the kitchen table, the "say something nice" rule was observed zealously at the Priest household.

We could use some of that same teaching and modeling today. Showing concern about others before we act or speak. Placing others' welfare before our own. Holding our tongue when we have the urge to be witty or sarcastic at someone's expense. And it all begins at your place of residence. We could use a "home remedy" to begin curing the rapidly spreading disease of Tact Deficit Disorder. The beginning of the end of TDD is found in your own home. Is there a doctor in the house?

✦ ✦ ✦

5

Lucky Jack

Full of excitement, Jack exploded through the front door and into the kitchen. He had just returned from his high school tennis match, and his words tumbled over each other as he spoke animatedly about the day's events. He'd done well in both the singles and doubles matches, and his team had won in the overall standings. But best of all, Jack found some money, in the grass, under the bleachers, at the tennis club where the matches had been played. For a high school junior, finding $150 was a big event and Jack had already spent the money in his mind.

As his dad listened to Jack's story, the facts became a bit clearer. While sitting in the bleachers, waiting for his turn to play, Jack looked down through the bleachers to the ground below and saw a clear sack filled with something that looked like money. Jack climbed down to investigate and, sure enough, it was a plastic bag filled with small bills totaling $150. Jack quickly stashed the package in his tennis bag. What luck! There were several things he'd been wanting to buy, and this plastic bag was his ticket to purchase them. In fact, Jack had already stopped on the way home and bought something with some of "his" new money. Jack thought to himself "I'm a lucky guy!"

Jack's dad had mixed emotions as he heard about the find. He was glad for Jack, but he knew what had to be done—and he knew it wouldn't be a popular idea with Jack. But he remembered his own dad telling him how dads weren't in the popularity business and when Jack finally calmed down enough to listen, Dad began to speak.

"Jack, I'm really happy for you," he began. "But there's a little unfinished business that has to be taken care of before you can call that money yours. It's possible the person who lost that money will be looking for it at the tennis club. You need to call the tennis club office and tell them you found a bag of money under the bleachers. If someone comes looking for it and can describe the amount of money in the bag, you'll need to give it back."

Jack looked both surprised and stunned. "Give it back?" he gasped. "You've got to be kidding. I found it and now it's mine—finders keepers." But Dad was insistent. "It's not 'finders keepers' unless no one comes to claim it. Until then, I'll hold onto it for you. Now, you'd better make that call to the club."

"This is unbelievable," cried Jack. "You're the only person in the world who would do something like this."

"I don't think that's true," said his dad. "But even if I were the only person, I would still do it because it's the right thing to do."

Reluctantly, Jack handed the bag over to his dad. Jack had seen that look of conviction in his father's eyes enough to know there was no talking him out of it. Then he dejectedly called the club and told them about his find. No one had reported any lost money yet, said the club manager, but if they did he'd call Jack right away. And before hanging up, he thanked Jack for his honesty.

"How long do I have to wait?" Jack asked his dad. "Oh, I'd say thirty days should be long enough," Dad replied. "If no one has claimed it by then, it's yours to keep."

The thirty days crawled by at a glacial pace. Every day of silence from the club was another day of relief to Jack. Finally, after the thirtieth day passed with no one laying claim to the money, Jack's dad declared him the new owner of $150 and an old plastic bag. Jack really was a lucky guy.

But not just lucky to find some money. That little bit of luck didn't last more than a few days before it was spent. Jack was lucky enough to have a dad who made a difference, a dad who put principle above popularity. A dad whose refusal to compromise honesty made him do seemingly silly things that "no one else in the world" would do. Jack found something he wasn't looking for when he found that lost bag of money. He found honesty and integrity in a plastic sack under a bleacher at the tennis club. Jack really was a lucky guy. Wouldn't it be great if all our children could be this lucky?

How do we pass along Jack's luck? By teaching and modeling that the little things really do count. Small compromises of our honesty and integrity don't seem very important at the time, but they're the predictable and dangerous prelude to further deterioration of our convictions. Each time we dilute our commitment to honesty, we're mixing a toxic drink that will poison us, our families, and our country. C.S. Lewis said it best, "The surest path to hell is not the sudden drop off, but the gentle slope under foot, without warnings and without signs." We're not often tempted to rob banks or embezzle hundreds of thousands of dollars.

Instead, each day we face a dozen small temptations to compromise. To avoid the gentle slope underfoot we must be
vigilant to guard against even small compromises to our
honesty and integrity.

It isn't luck that keeps us honest—it's conviction, and action based on that conviction. Let's decide among ourselves
that we'll make the difficult, sometimes seemingly insig-
nificant choices to be honest in even the smallest things.
Let's pass along a little of Jack's luck to our children.

✦ ✦ ✦

6

Humble Yourselves

The Father's Day Sunday Oklahoman sports page featured an article about Tulsa Hurricane football coach Dave Rader. I don't know Mr. Rader, but I liked what I read. He seems to work hard at balancing a demanding career as a college football coach with the equally demanding job of being a father. But the one Rader quality I especially liked was his humility.

Rader doesn't have a reserved parking space at the University's athletic complex. When asked what he does for a living he simply tells folks, "I work at the University of Tulsa." Every year he goes to his church's Christmas break retreat for 5th and 6th graders to sweep floors and wipe tables. The writer of the column described him as a man with "an ego in check."

The children's pastor at his church said it best. "I love him doing things with the kids. I like for them to see that example. He never thinks he's too good to take out the trash. He's a very humble man."

Humble? That's an odd sounding word, isn't it? We don't often associate humility with successful people like Dave Rader. It's even more unusual to see it modeled on a consistent basis. Like in our homes. But I'm convinced it's an imperative for well balanced lives and families.

While it's true successful people have self-confidence, there has to be a balance between appropriate confidence and appropriate humility. Being humble doesn't require you to be a Casper Milquetoast or display an "aw shucks" attitude. Being humble simply requires an accurate self-concept.

The New Testament book of Romans gives us a hint about how to achieve the delicate balance between being overly humble and overly proud. "I say to every person among you not to think more highly of himself than he ought to think, but to think so as to have sound judgment" (Romans 12:3). The Apostle Paul is telling us not to think too highly of ourselves, but don't think too lowly of ourselves either. We should think about ourselves—and our family members—with sound judgment.

In our achievement-oriented world we sometimes think humble people will never be noticed. We're afraid someone will overlook us if we don't toot our own horn. By words and example we often show our families the opinion that the humble person gets left behind. We need to display humility in our own lives, in our homes and in our conversations with others. We even need to be modest about the accomplishments of family members. Too much bragging is an ugly thing.

Of course there is an opposite danger. Zig Ziglar notes that for every positive, affirming word spoken in the average American home, ten negative words are uttered. Too often family members are reminded of their limitations. "Don't try that, you'll get hurt." "You'll never make it through that class." "You know nobody in our family is good at that." By voicing such defeatist talk about family members' goals, we almost insure their failure. This kind of home life produces people who lack self-confidence. Both a lack of self-confidence and a lack of humility are unhealthy.

How then do we achieve this balance Paul talks about? How do we think with "sound judgment"?

Encourage healthy self-concept in your home. Verbally affirm the good things your family members do, especially admirable character qualities they display. You might even write a note telling them how proud you are of them.

Lead by example. Show your family by example that a certain amount of self-confidence is essential, but constantly dwelling on yourself is destructive and defeating. Bragging makes you a person shunned by others. People avoid a self-made man who's in love with his creator.

Remember humility is not a wimpy virtue. Moses, the famous liberator of the Jews from Egyptian slavery, was reported to have been the humblest man alive. We sure don't think about Moses being a wimp, do we? Humility is a strong virtue to cultivate.

Humble yourself. Take affirmative steps to be a person of humility. Wipe off the table or take out the trash. Try to avoid talking about yourself. Adopt the attitude of a servant. The New Testament book of James tells us to "Humble ourselves in the sight of the Lord and at the proper time He will exalt you." Our part is to be humble. God's part is to exalt us at the proper time. Don't get the two roles mixed up.

Humility can't be effectively taught by words alone. It must be modeled in our homes. A humble, self-confident person is a rare creature indeed, but it's the kind of person our families need to see.

✢ ✢ ✢

7

Charity Begins at Home

It was recently revealed that Vice President Al Gore contributed only about $300 last year to charitable organizations. With his large salary, this chintzy charitable contribution earned him the nickname, "The Cheap Veep." Rightly so. In an era where "looking out for No. 1" is a popular sentiment, it is absolutely imperative for our leaders—and our families—to display a giving spirit.

This idea hit home with me during a discussion with one of my children. They related a recent talk with a friend about allowances. The conversation went something like this:

> *"How do you spend your allowance?"*
> *"I tithe ten percent, I save ten percent and then I spend the rest on gifts or whatever else I want or need."*
> *"What's a 'tithe'?"*

My own child was stunned to find out not everyone is familiar with the idea of tithing—giving 10% of your income back to the good Lord who gave it to you. Clearly, this friend wasn't in the habit of that kind of charitable giving.

Maybe the friend's family was unfamiliar with tithing but practiced charitable giving in other ways. I hope so. Because it is through our giving back to the community that we make eternal investments. It is in giving that we reap our own reward. We should give because there is a need. We should give because we ought. But when the need and the ought mix together and prompt generous action, the result is a warm glow of fulfillment that can't be matched in any other way. We are happiest ourselves when we contribute to the needs of others.

It's that kind of mentality which we must cultivate in our families. That giving spirit must be both modeled and taught in our homes. If we expect our children to be positive contributors to our communities (both of time and money) we must be contributors ourselves, and we must affirmatively teach our children how to do it. Where do we begin? Try these steps in your own family, and be sure to include your children in the giving process.

First, we should be prudent with our charitable investments. Carefully evaluate where your time and money should go. Be sure you believe in the organization's mission. The people carrying out that mission should possess integrity and commitment. Review annual statements and assure yourself that the church, synagogue or charity is on-task and on-target. Both our time and our money must be carefully invested in the right charitable causes.

We should be modest in the way we give. The New Testament teaches that we should give in an unassuming way. Jesus contrasted the quiet, sacrificial giving of the widow with the pompous, self-aggrandizing giving of the Pharisees. If we give for show or acclaim, Jesus said that we "already have our reward," but if we give from the heart, without fanfare, we will be "rewarded in heaven." How we give is more important than how much we give.

We should seldom repress a generous impulse. I heard this phrase several years ago, and it has stuck, glue-like, in my mind ever since. As far as it is within our abilities, we should give when we are internally prompted to do so. Granted, we should not be foolish and give to a charity when our own home is in dire need. But the more frequently generous impulses are suppressed, the less frequently they will come. Soon the heart turns cold. We want warm hearts in our homes, not stony ones.

We should give consistently. The concept of tithe has a number of benefits. One is that it promotes consistent, scheduled giving. Sure, we should feel free to give spontaneously when led to do so, but we should also give in a regular, predictable way. With tithing, the "first fruits" of your labor are offered back to God. In the Old Testament the tithe was 10% of all your income, whether that was farm produce, livestock or money. Writing a check or depositing cash in the offering takes on new significance when it's done each pay period in a predictable manner. A regular, reliable contributor is a "God send" to charitable organizations, and tithing or regular giving promotes "ownership" of the mission.

We should give gladly. The Bible says the Lord loves a cheerful giver, and even the largest, most generous gift loses impact if it is given begrudgingly. Don't give till it hurts, give till it feels good. Model in your family the face of a happy person investing in eternal values.

It's true that charity begins at home, but it should not end there. Foster a charitable conscience in yourself and your family. It's an investment that pays generous dividends that can't be measured. ✛

8

Grow Up!
Avoiding the Blame Game

San Francisco Mayor Willie Brown was steamed, and it ended up getting him in hot water for shooting off his mouth. It seems the San Francisco 49er football team and their back-up quarterback, Elvis Grbac, lost a game Willie Brown thought they should have won. Interviewed the next day, Mayor Brown announced that Grbac was "an embarrassment to humankind," and that he wouldn't let Grbac play in the new 49er stadium about to be built. Hot words from a hot head. Of course, the words stung even more because Grbac and his wife Lori had recently learned that their son had spina bifida. Grbac's concern for his son had probably affected his play in the game. When Brown belatedly learned this piece of news, he was understandably regretful about his unfeeling and unthinking remarks. "I don't know if he'll (Grbac) accept my apology or whether he'll forgive me, but I hope he will," Brown later apologized. Grbac said he would, but the wounding words still hurt.

Contrast Brown's attitude of "Ready-Fire-Aim" with that of former British Prime Minister William Gladstone. In preparing for an important speech before Parliament, Gladstone asked an employee at the Treasury to compile some financial statistics for use in the presentation. Gladstone had confidence in the employee's work and gave the oration without checking the accuracy of the figures. It turned out the employee had made a serious mistake and, as a result, Gladstone gave erroneous information, exposing him to ridicule and embarrassment before the Parliament.

Gladstone immediately sent for the man who compiled the statistics. As the employee entered the office full of fear and sure of his firing, Gladstone greeted him warmly. "I know how much you must be disturbed by what has happened and I have sent for you to put you at your ease. For a long time you have been engaged in handling the intricacies of the national accounts and this is the first mistake you've made. I want to congratulate you and express to you my keen appreciation." Then he shook the hand of the dumb-founded and relieved employee. The man must have felt like he was pardoned from a certain death.

Many times we resemble Willie Brown more than we do William Gladstone. Whether we've lost a game or lost face, it seems that embarrassment makes us want to play the "blame game." We point an accusing finger at someone else and say, "That guy over there is the reason for this mess!" We want to distance ourselves from the fall-out of fault and be sure to announce to the world that it wasn't us who caused the problem. Like Willie Brown, we assign blame and self-righteously pass judgment, often without knowing the full story. Willie Brown could learn something from William Gladstone. So could we.

Are we fast to find fault at our work or in our family? Quick to criticize? Rapid in our rebukes? Do we follow the "shoot from the lip" example of Willie Brown or the forgiving fig-ure of William Gladstone? The Brown-like response is easier and more natural. Like little kids playing the game "hot potato," we do our best at work to avoid holding the blame bag. If we can pass it along to someone else, we quickly do so by passing along a critical comment or two. This torched-tongue approach is especially evident in our homes when we let down our guard and abandon our good manners. It is tempting to lash out at some slight, error, or "injustice" we've endured at the hands of another family member. Like Willie Brown, we shoot first and ask questions later.

But the Gladstone model is how *we'd* like to be treated by others. And it's how we, at our better moments, should treat others. We should refrain from blaming others at work—whether or not they're truly to blame. We ought to treat family members at least as well as we treat those outside the home. We ought to be considerate of the feelings of others whether they are down the street, across the factory floor or linked to us by the bonds of love, blood or marriage.

Where can we begin the process of treating other people with civility? The answer is on the tip of our tongue. Proverbs 10:19 says, "A wise person restrains his lips." Those words are as true today as they were thousands of years ago when Solomon first wrote them. According to James 1:19, we ought to be quick to hear, slow to speak, and slow to anger. The Lord gave us two ears and one mouth, and we should use them in that proportion.

We can learn a lesson from the "tale of two Wills." Don't be a Willie Brown. Instead, be a William Gladstone. We should avoid the blame game and keep our words sweet. Tomorrow we may have to eat them.

family talk

Family

≈ family talk

9

Reflections on
Gram's Funeral

Nellie Raymond, my maternal grandmother, died April 8, 1990. She was the mother of ten proud children and the grandmother of a score or more. She passed away in her sleep just a few days after celebrating her 90th birthday with 40 of the family-faithful. I didn't make it to the party. She lived in Pennsylvania. I live in Oklahoma. I am a lawyer. It would have been expensive and hard to get off work to fly out there for the party, or so I thought. Two days later though, when I heard of her death, I cleared a week of appointments, got court permission to reschedule a trial, and bought an airline ticket to fly out and be with the family for the funeral. It's too bad funerals sometimes seem more important than birthdays.

I flew to Syracuse, New York, my hometown, and picked up my parents and sister for the three-hour drive to the small town of Port Allegheny, Pennsylvania where Gram lived for over half a century. It was the place I spent many summer vacations catching crawdads in the stream and trying out all my grandpa's hats, which hung on hooks in the garage. I used to wander into Grandpa's carpenter shop to hear the sound of his tools, smell the sawdust and listen to Grandpa's stories of days gone by.

I remember being a young boy and walking down to Main Street with Gram to visit the Market Basket grocery store, the hardware store or the Dry Goods store, where clerks would always say, "So you're Nellie's grandson." Everyone knew Nellie. She was a woman who's strongest exclamation of anger was "Bean soup" or "Lord, give me strength." She whistled all the time, whether she was making Johnny cakes for breakfast or blackberry pie from the berries we picked together in the woods. Her pies were so sweet I often ate too much and got sick.

Once, after I was grown up and living in Oklahoma, I went back east on business. I had some work to do in western Pennsylvania and decided to take some extra time and spend the night with Gram. Grandpa had passed on by this time, and she lived alone in the pink house on Maple Street. She must have been in her 80's at that time. She cooked supper for us. Roast beef and potatoes and tomatoes. She'd picked the tomatoes out of her backyard just like she'd done so many times through the years. Out in her backyard where we had played croquet, where I had swung on the wooden swing Grandpa put up, where he and I had looked for nightcrawlers to go fishing. There were a lot of memories in that backyard. After supper we sat out back for awhile and talked.

It was different being at her house that night, just the two of us. No other family around to distract us. We just talked about days past and croquet games won and lost. It happened to be a Wednesday night so we went to mid-week prayer service at her church—just as she always did. We walked just down the street to the Evangelical United Brethren Church, as we had done so many times before. That night she introduced me to everyone as her grandson *the preacher*. I tried to tell her quietly, on the side, that I was a lawyer. She just nodded, smiled and said, "Uh huh," and basically ignored what I was saying. So that night I was her grandson, the preacher.

When I drove away from her house the next day, and watched her wave good-bye from the driveway I knew I was waving good-bye to an era of my life. It made me a little sad to know I wouldn't be back to catch crawdads, look for earthworms, eat Johnny cakes or play croquet. Like a wonderful book I loved to re-read but couldn't find in the library anymore, those times were going to simply be memories now.

A few years later she passed away. As it turned out, I gave the eulogy at her funeral service because there was a new preacher at Grandma's church, and he hadn't known her all that long. I ended up preaching a little sermon about what heaven must be like now that Gram was there.

Maybe Gram knew something I didn't that Wednesday night, years earlier, when she introduced me to her friends at church as her grandson the preacher. I ended up being the preacher at her funeral after all. I wonder how she knew. But Grandmas are like that, you know. They seem to know things that the rest of us only guess about. It's definitely worth the time to get to know them and learn about their lives, their wisdom, their view of the world. Make sure you take the time to get to know your grandmother—or grandfather before it's too late. And be sure your kids know theirs too. Connecting the generations makes for close-knit families. It's like building a bridge to the past.

Grandma Raymond's Eulogy

I wonder what heaven is like now that Gram is there.

I'll bet it's a lot like it was here in Port Allegheny when she was around.

I'll bet they're eating better in heaven today. They're probably having roast beef and mashed potatoes and blackberry pie for supper and Johnny cakes and bacon for breakfast, 'cause that's what Gram is probably fixing for them, just like she fixed it for us when she was here.

She probably had them go out to the woods and pick berries with a pail or a coffee can tied with a rope around their angelic waists so they could pick two-handed. Can't you just see that? White-robed angels getting blackberry stains on themselves. I wonder if they'll eat too much pie and get sick like I always did.

And I'll bet there's more whistlin' in heaven today because Gram's there, just like she used to whistle in the kitchen when she was cooking. I remember coming down the stairs from the attic bedroom in the morning and hearing that whistling floating up to my ears. That meant Gram was up and breakfast would soon be sitting in front of me. Heaps of pancakes and butter and syrup filling my plate and the smell of bacon grease filling my nostrils as I ate and ate and ate. Why, I'll bet heaven even smells of bacon grease now.

I'll bet they're playing more croquet in heaven today, just like we did with Gram when she was here. She'll be out there in the backyard of one of the Bible heroes, beating the pants off all of them just like she used to do to us. I can just see her hitting the green ball belonging to the Apostle Paul. She'll probably send him flying down into the neighbor's flower patch, just like she used to do to me. I wonder if he'll get as mad and frustrated as I did. Seems like she always won. I'll bet she's winning up there too.

I'll bet heaven is a better place now that Gram's there. They're eating better and whistling more and playing more croquet than they used to before she arrived. It's more the kind of place I want to be someday because heaven is now the kind of place it was around here when Gram was with us. With Gram in heaven it kind of gives new meaning to the expression "going home," doesn't it? And when we finally do get there I'll bet she'll be waiting to greet us at the pearly gates just like she did when we pulled into her driveway in Port. She'll be walking down that street of gold, wiping her hands on her apron, with a bit of flour on her face or in her hair, ready to give us a hug and a kiss.

I'm looking forward to heaven a little bit more, now that Gram's there.

10

Humor in the Home

I felt a whack on the side of my face, and I knew I was in trouble. My mother had hit me again. It was becoming a ritual around our house, and I knew I had to get her back. I hid and quietly waited for her to walk by so I could ambush her. Then, when she least expected it, I struck. I reared back my arm and let it fly, striking her right in the forehead. Boom! A direct hit! But before I could take too much pleasure in my great triumph she was after me again. It seemed I could never escape her deadly aim with those pancakes!

Pancakes? Yep, pancakes. It was a tradition around my house to end every pancake breakfast with a "pancake fight." My mother learned this epic game from her mother and passed the legacy on to us. We'd take those leftover, "starting to get hard" pancakes, divide them among our family members and then have a good old fashioned free-for-all. The rules were: 1) you couldn't go into the dining room where we had good wallpaper, 2) you couldn't use any pancakes that had butter or syrup on them, and 3) you had to help clean up the pancake scraps after the "war" was over. Other than that it was open season, and we would have a fun-filled time throwing pancakes at each other, chasing around the house until the pancakes gave out or we did. This is just one of many memories of home-made fun we had around our house as I was growing up. And the tradition lives on. We still have pancake fights at our house today.

Our homes ought to be places of fun, where humor is found daily and laughter is heard often. Sure there are chores to do, bills to be paid, serious things to discuss. But if our homes and families aren't marked by fun and laughter we're unlikely to find it anywhere else in our lives.

Humor and laughing are good for you. Norman Cousins, former editor of *The Saturday Evening Post* made laughter a prescriptive medicine with his book, *Anatomy of an Illness,* in which he recounted how laughter healed him from a life-threatening disease that doctors had pronounced incurable. We know that laughter is good exercise—it increases our pulse, works our hearts, and generally makes us feel better. What *Reader's Digest* says each month is true–laughter *is* the best medicine.

Even if humor didn't have all these healthy aspects I would still advocate it because laughter makes family life more enjoyable. Children pick up on the presence or absence of humor in our homes. As a result, they tend to become humor-filled or humor-less people. If you've ever looked around and seen a grumpy face, you know you don't want your children turning out like that! Laughter also enriches a marriage. It bonds partners together. It creates "memory moments" you can pull from your mind and replay for years to come. No doubt about it—laughter makes for strong families.

You may protest—"But I'm not a good joke teller" or "I'm just not a funny person." No excuses accepted. We're all funny people. Just look in the mirror first thing in the morning if you doubt it. There are lots of different ways to inject humor into our family bloodstream, and you don't have to be a Jay Leno or a David Letterman to do it. Try some of these:

- Read the comic strips in the newspaper every morning. Clip a good one and post it on your refrigerator door or leave it for a family member with a note telling them it made you think of them.

- Buy a funny calendar. Try the Far Side® daily calendar or Joke-a-Day calendar. Even if only half of the daily jokes or cartoons are funny, you'll still be laughing at least 180 times more in the next year.

- Don't take yourself too seriously. Learn to see humor in your life, and don't be afraid to laugh at yourself when you do something dumb. Relish re-telling the story of an embarrassing moment. One of my family's favorites is when I mistakenly used the ladies' restroom and had to sneak out before I was seen!

- Check out funny books or joke books from your local library. It doesn't cost anything and even if you can't tell a good joke, you can at least read one to a fellow family member.

- Come up with wild and silly traditions—like the pancake fight. Or water wars. Or "crazy hat night." Be creative. Try sitting at different places at the supper table and pretend you're the person who usually sits there. Little brother gets to be "dad" and mom acts like she's the teen-age sister. Remember, don't take yourself too seriously and don't get your feelings hurt if someone portrays you accurately!

Begin tonight to make your home a house of laughter. Look for the lunacy in life and enjoy it. Who knows? Maybe you'll get a chance to whack someone in the head with a pancake!

✢ ✢ ✢

11

Family Mealtime is Important

I still remember that summer evening in 1976. I was a college kid working in Philadelphia, Pennsylvania and a newfound friend, Scottie, had invited me to his home for dinner. We hit the door just as the food was being placed on the table. Quick introductions were made all around, and we sat down to eat. Then it happened.

Scott's dad turned on the television. All family member's eyes were glued to the nightly news. For the next twenty minutes the only sound heard around the table was the scrape of forks against plates and the droning of the TV newsman. No one talked around the table; we simply ate, watched the news and when the telecast was over, each family member flew off in different directions. It was a family dinner, but we hadn't really shared a meal together. We just happened to all be eating at the same table.

That meal was quite a contrast to the family meals I knew. Around our supper table there was usually lively conversation. Stories about the day's events. Troubles to sort out. Victories to relive. Plans to be made. Chores to be assigned. I must admit not all our family meals were "made for TV" quality. Sometimes we were angry, or sad, or depressed. But we shared our lives around the family meal, and we fed our bodies and our spirits at the supper table.

There are many benefits to eating meals together as a family. Children who share family meals do better in school and on achievement tests than children who don't, according to Jan Carpenter of the University of Illinois at Champaign-Urbana. The key is not the eating, says Carpenter, it's the emotional support and time spent together that helps. And children learn organizational skills during meal time. All this helps in school.

There's more. Ellyn Satter, a therapist at the Family Therapy Center in Madison, Wisconsin, says family meals are an important rest stop in our fast-paced society. Even though it's hard to get a meal on and get the family to the table, Satter contends that it's worth the effort. "Kids need the parenting *and* the nutrition," says Satter. "Family meals are an essential part of parenting—part of the structure that every family needs to function."

Even if it seems virtually impossible to get your herd together for grazing at the kitchen table, you should give it your best try. Here's some suggestions that might help:

Tell your family that family meals are important and they will be held on a regular basis. Just getting everyone together to agree on that may be a feat. But once you establish meal time as a priority, you have a basis to work from. It may require some schedule juggling or readjustment. But as Satter says, it's worth the effort.

Keep the conversation pleasant and light and include everyone in the discussions. Mealtime is not the place for scolding, discipline or heated arguments. Deal with those issues later. Make the dinner table a place family members want to sit around, not avoid.

Don't get hung up on "eating right." Many a family meal has been spoiled by a fight between parent and child over asparagus. Lighten up! No child in America has starved to death when good food was available. Satter, who is also a registered dietitian, says there should be a division of labor at mealtime. Parents decide what to serve and children decide how much or little they eat. Satter says she's found that the nutritional quality of a child's diet will average out pretty well over time. If they don't want to eat the good food that's served, that's fine. But no dessert. And the next meal is breakfast, so no snacks in between. Kids will get the message if you hold the line on this approach. Believe me, they won't starve.

Expect good behavior at mealtime and excuse children from the table if they don't behave. Satter says that being at the family table is a privilege, and the meal should be pleasant for everyone—parents included. Good manners and proper eating etiquette are best taught at the family dinner. Use the opportunity to "civilize" the barbarians.

Be flexible about the process. Maybe a family dinner doesn't fit your schedule. Then make it a breakfast or a lunch. Can't find time to cook a meal? No problem. Gather everyone around a fast food restaurant table. There's no hard and fast rule in this game other than "just do it."

Family meals are more than just a time to gather around a common plate of food and watch TV. Let your meal times as a family be regular, fun and meaningful. You may throw away the leftovers, but you'll keep the memories forever.

12

Families that Succeed

I have a friend who is a successful attorney in another town. He's also a successful dad. Neither thing happened by accident. He has a good law practice because he built it carefully, with integrity and skill. He has a good family because he took seriously his role as father and husband. I recently asked him if he had any "keys to success" in raising a family, and the things he told me sounded a lot like the things I heard years ago in a speech by Dr. Jay Kessler, former president of Youth for Christ International and current president of Taylor University in Indiana. Here's what Dr. Kessler and my friend had to say about "families that succeed":

Families that succeed are families where love is openly evident between husband and wife, parent and child. There should be no shame or reluctance to openly display affection toward those we love. Everyone has their own way to show love. Some people are huggers, others are ear nibblers and some just hold hands, but no spouse or child should have to spend very much time wondering if they are loved. Show them. It is especially important for children to see their parents display affection toward one another. There is no greater gift you can give your child than to openly show love to your spouse.

You should also freely express affection for your children no matter their age. Teens need to be treated a bit differently than toddlers, but the same principle applies: find a way to show and tell them you love them. Touch them, hug them, rub their head or pat their hand, but whatever you do find a way to openly express your love.

Families that succeed are families where respect for each individual is assured. Whether parent or child, younger or older, each individual in the family should be treated with respect. In talking about respect, Kessler paid Billy Graham a compliment in reporting that Graham had never entered any of his children's bedrooms without first knocking on the door. Graham respected their privacy, and we should do the same with our family members.

Kessler said that he always required his family members to show respect for one another by using each other's given name when they were in a disagreement. It's easier to treat someone impersonally and less humanely if you refer to them in the third person, "*He* did that or *she* did this." If you call someone by the third person you can put them in a "bag" and do them in. So Kessler made everyone call one another by their personal name. "*Jack,* you did that or *Jamie,* you did this." It's harder to "bag" someone and show them disrespect when you call them by name.

Families that succeed are families where rules and boundaries are understood and communicated. My lawyer/friend was big on this one. He told me the "no" of a parent has to be meaningful. It has to be enforced. And it has to make sense. Parents should ask themselves if there is a purpose behind their "no." Say yes as much as you can, and reserve your "no" for things that are important. And when you say no, be sure that any transgressions are punished. My friend told me about his son, a senior in high school, who recently said to his mother "You've taken all the peer-pressure heat off me, Mom. Everyone knows you've laid down the rules about drinking and stuff. They know I just can't do it." This mom's "no" meant something.

Families that succeed are families committed to "process." Kessler reminded us that the girl or boy you're raising isn't going to "freeze" in their current condition. They're in the process of maturing, so be sure to give them a little time. "He's going through a phase." is a true statement that can lessen a lot of parental anxiety. But by the same token the "phase philosophy" shouldn't be used as an escape or a cop-out when training or correction is needed. Children are like tender plants growing in your garden. You have to give them support, water and nurture them, but most importantly, give them time to grow.

Finally, families that succeed are families where God is the head of the household. Some families are into a power struggle. Dad tries to rule with an iron fist. Mom tries to seize control. Kids subvert and thwart the efforts of the parents. But when everyone is subject to the sovereignty of God there's less time spent in power struggles. This is not to say that these successful families never wrangle with the power issue or have disagreements about who's in charge. It's just that ultimately, with a proper reminder, these families realize they are all subject to the same Head of the house.

Both Jay Kessler and my lawyer/friend made a lot of sense, and they helped remind me of the things I need to focus on. Success in the family. It doesn't come about by accident. You have to work at it.

13

Encountering Tragedy

Young and talented and pretty. Those were the words most often used to describe the sixteen-year-old, blond-headed girl who had a life full of promise stretched out before her. But without warning, she fell unexplainably ill. It was the middle of the night, and she could not sleep. Restless and feverish she tossed back and forth in bed until her parents were awakened and came to sit by her side. She laid her head in her mother's lap and after feeling the soft stroke of her mother's hand on her hair, she became quite silent. In a rare moment that neither doctors nor science fully comprehended, she slipped off her mortal robe and moved heavenward. Frantic calls to doctors and the wail of emergency vehicles could not call her back. Before she had left home, she had left earth.

In the days that followed her death, I observed the young girl's family experience profound grief. But their grief had an unmistakable nobility to it. The family drew close, friends drew near, and they all drew strength from God. This family handled tragedy with more poise, dignity and inner peace than I feared I would possess in the same circumstance. Awkwardly I offered my sympathies, knowing I could not know how they felt. But the grace with which they lived those days—and the many days since—has been a source of inspiration and encouragement to me and to many others. Even now, as I see them living their lives with a smile and with joy, I continue to be amazed at their reliance on God and their personal perseverance. And as I pray for them I pray for myself as well, that when I encounter tragedy I should live as well as they.

Every family encounters with tragedy. We lose a loved one to death, someone suffers a discouraging illness, a job is lost, a house burns down, a child is born with a serious birth defect. It is inevitable that each family will face some grief-producing event, but what is not so predictable is whether the tragedy will tear the family apart or knit it together even more tightly. Statistics confirm that within a year of losing a child to death many, many parents divorce. Yet still others, faced with such a loss, learn to persevere and see their marriages strengthened.

What determines how a family handles tragedy? Certainly there are a multitude of variables, but there seem to be several common characteristics of families who survive and often emerge stronger from the refining fire of adversity.

Families that endure through tragedy have a faith in God. Professor Nick Stinnet, in a study of "strong families" conducted several years ago, found that a common religious faith marked families who endure. While much effort has been made in the past few decades to keep church separate from state, the fact remains that faith and family should be inseparable. Can a family be close-knit and successful without a religious faith? Undoubtedly there are some who can. But the odds of developing a persevering family are greatly enhanced when members are united in a common faith.

Families that endure through tragedy are outwardly focused. While they deal with the tragedy at hand they remember they are not the only ones suffering, nor are they the only ones with needs. The enduring family does not permit self-pity to swallow them up, they don't continually nurse the old wounds, and they don't spend most of their time bemoaning their tragedy to anyone who will listen. These persevering families keep their chin up by looking up and looking out. They seek to minister to others experiencing trials. They are willing to share their secrets of coping. In a phrase they are *selfless, not self-centered.*

Finally, families that endure learn to embrace the pain. They are willing to talk about their situation if it will help someone else. They grieve appropriately over their loss and allow the tears to flow. They open their circle of intimate agony and are graceful in receiving the love and concern offered by sympathetic friends. It is often easier to help others in need than it is to allow others to help you, but these enduring families learn to humbly permit solace to be given. And they talk about their tragedy with a refreshing openness that results from reflection. They have thought about their tragedy, and they are learning from it. They do not wallow in misery but are wise enough to let their feelings come out and allow the healing to begin through the balm of loving conversation.

Tragedy will befall each family. None of us will live an unblemished life. But the family that best endures adversity has a common faith, an outward focus and an acceptance of the pain. Begin today to lay the foundation for a family that will endure and even grow through tragedy. Develop the family bonds of common faith, outward focus and appropriate intimacy before tragedy befalls. It's never too early to prepare for our inevitable encounters with the stumbling blocks of life. But properly prepared, we can use stumbling blocks for stepping stones to a higher plane of family unity.

✝ ✝ ✝

14

Be a Bread Maker

I remember well the smell of fresh baked bread wafting across my nine-year-old nostrils as I entered my house after school. My mom was a bread maker, and her fresh rolls and bread were enough to make any young boy come straight home from school regardless of the tempting mischief that might try to sidetrack him. The aroma of her bread was only slightly surpassed by the delicious taste of it as I wrapped my mouth around an oven-warm slice, blanketed with butter. Mmmmmm.

So in an effort to relive my childhood, I have become a bread maker too. At first I thought I could "save time" and shortcut the process with one of those new fangled bread machines. But I soon found out that both the process and the product were less than my hopes and dreams. The machine did save me time—but that was part of what I didn't like. It let me loose too quickly, and it didn't require me to get my hands messy. The whole process was too neat, too easy, and the bread that emerged after the dictated incubation period didn't match my expectations. So I decided to go back to the original recipe.

I opened the old recipe box and found the index card with my mother's handwritten notes about making homemade bread. Even though making bread the old-fashioned way takes a good chunk of time, I found it to be a welcome change of pace from my usually hurried world. Like a scenic turnout along the highway my bread-making times provide a chance to slow down, reflect a bit and enjoy the smell of nostalgia. I look forward to greasing my hands so I can knead the dough, pushing and pulling and slapping at the large lump of flour mixed with egg and water. As I work the bread I can remember my mom with a kerchief on her head, kneading the dough and holding it up for inspection. Then she'd slap the dough down again and turn it over and over on the flour-spattered counter of our kitchen. She never looked like she was in a hurry, and she always had time to talk with me as she worked. I don't remember exactly what we talked about, but they were easy-going conversations— unrushed and ambling—like a walk down a country road.

Now I knead my dough and set it in a bowl to rise for thirty minutes while I find something else to do that isn't too absorbing. You can't get too involved in anything else or stray too far from the kitchen because the bread won't let you get away. It's not like those bread machines. Baking bread the right way demands some attention; but it's not too demanding—like a boiling pot of minute rice might be. You can do some slow-paced things while the bread rises, like talking casually with your kids or writing your mom a letter—something that takes *some* attention, but allows you to keep a half watchful eye on the rising or baking dough.

I like waiting for the bread to rise and bake. I think it must be because the bread beckons me backward to a slower era. It calls me to a time when a homey kitchen contained a warm-hearted mother baking bread the old-fashioned way. When a nine-year-old boy could wrap his mouth around two or three slices of fresh bread and never give a second thought to "fat content" or "caloric intake."

I know we can't live in the past, but it's nice to go back and visit once in a while. Maybe that's why I'll always be a bread maker. And maybe that's why I want to teach my children how to bake bread the old-fashioned way. Telling our children the stories of our youth and the traditions of our past reveals a part of us to them which they need to see. It gives them a sense of history, of belonging. And spending time with them in an old-fashioned, slow-paced, bread-making way is a fool-proof way to connect with them soul to soul.

There's undoubtedly some activity, some tradition of your past you could share and re-live with your children. Why not slow down long enough to give them a family history lesson they won't soon forget? Bake bread with your children.

15

Write a Letter, Save a Letter

She pulled out several big boxes which had been stashed way in the back of her closet, behind the out-of-season clothes. When she blew the dust off and opened them, I didn't know quite what to expect. She carefully lifted out a large, photograph-album-looking book and painstakingly began separating the pages—and as she did so I saw years of love and heartache, joy and sadness, news and gossip spill out of the pages of that book.

It was a book filled with old letters from family members, dating back to the early 1900s. My mother-in-law had carefully preserved them for the edification of future generations. "I'm not the owner—just the keeper of these letters" she reminded us. "They belong to the whole family, and anyone can borrow them to read anytime they like."

So I sat down for awhile and peeked over the shoulder of those who had gone before, reading what they wrote about trips to St. Louis and trips into town, state fairs and scarlet fever, baby births and cantankerous cousins. It was like stepping through a looking glass into another generation. I heard the creak of buggy wheels and the clip clop of horse hooves down the streets of Burkburnett, Texas. I could smell fresh pecan pie and mashed potatoes at a family gathering. I felt perspiration roll down my face during a hot, north Texas summer. What a wonderful family treasure to pass along to the next generation: a glimpse of life in the family many years ago. It's a better inheritance than a pewter tea set.

Letter writing—and letter keeping—is too much of a lost art these days. It's easier for us to telephone relatives. Or e-mail them. Our communications are much too transitory and fleeting, and I fear our children and theirs will be the worse for it. Does anyone in your family take correspondence seriously? Do they write letters and answer correspondence when it comes in? Are letters from grandparents or aunts and uncles or brothers and sisters preserved so that when they're gone, some footprints will be left behind? I hope so. Maybe you could be the one in your family to work on this important part of preserving family legacy.

I love getting mail. I love going to the mailbox. When my friend Michael helped me install my e-mail program on my computer, he said, "This is great Jim. You'll never have to go out to the mailbox again!" I told Michael, "But I LIKE going out to the mailbox." I go out the front door, leap over the little wall and peer into the cavern-like box on the street to see if there's a written word connecting me to anyone out there. I like to get letters because it tells me someone cared enough to spend thirty-two cents and some of their precious time to draw me into their world. Letters connect me to my family far away.

And I've resolved this year that I'm going to write more letters to my family miles away. And I'm going to keep their letters when they write back. This collection of correspondence won't ever be as famous as the letters exchanged between Meriweather Lewis and President Thomas Jefferson during the exploration of the Louisiana Purchase, but it will mark my little corner of family history just the same.

You could do this for your family. Writing letters is a little bit like writing family history. You might even keep copies of your own letters as well as the ones you receive. Arrange them in an album for your kids to read in the years ahead. Make note of who wrote them and what their relationship is to your family. You'll be leaving an important part of yourself and your family history to future generations.

Letter writing is an endangered species. Don't let it become extinct. Get out your pen and paper. File away those letter gems you receive. Keep your family history alive for generations to come.

✢ ✢ ✢

16

Sharing Blackberries

Writer W.W. Meade tells the story of growing up in a hard-working family. His dad, a doctor by profession and a farmer by necessity, worked long hours, and most of the farm labor was left to his teen-age son. There was little time for laughing, joking or fooling around; there was too much work. But amidst all the work, the boy realized that his dad was pushing himself too hard. Long days at the office, nights filled with house calls and always, always, the interruption of supper with some emergency phone call.

The boy could see the toll it was taking on his father, and he tried to persuade his dad to take a few hours and get away for some fishing. Each time, the conscientious doctor would wave him off as he ran to help another needy person. But there were needs unmet right at home.

Finally, the teenager decided he had to get tough with his dad. One Friday he "bullied" him into going fishing at the family farm pond. They caught fish, cooked a meal and talked around an open camp fire. His dad looked young and happy and relaxed. Then while his father made a pot of coffee, the younger Meade went to the edge of a meadow and picked ripe blackberries into his baseball cap for their dessert. As the embers of the fire glowed, they shared blackberries, and the dad told his son how proud he was of him and how much he cared about him. Years later both dad and son would remember that night by the pond with fond remembrance, recalling how they had shared life and blackberries in an unhurried moment one quiet evening.

In our hectic-paced lives we don't spend many evenings sharing blackberries with our family, do we? It's not parents alone who are the busy ones. The schedules of children and teens can be dizzying as well. Ball games and scout meetings, band practices and gymnastics—not to mention civic groups, school and church functions. All these activities *can* be very good for both parents and their kids; but the good is often the worst enemy of the best. I have come to believe that all our busyness is not only maddening, it is menacing to a healthy lifestyle and homestyle. So like the anti-drug campaign message, we have to learn to "just say no" to too much busyness.

I find this very difficult to do. But if I am truly committed to building relationships in my home, I must maximize time with my family and minimize time spent elsewhere—even if this means saying no to things I'd like to do.

You can beat the beast of busyness. Take the vow of simplicity. Slow down, at least periodically, to lay in the grass with your children, take a walk with your spouse by the lake or talk leisurely after supper with your family. True, there are many worthy activities calling you away from home, just as those sick people called Doctor Meade. But there are voices closer to home you must heed. Place a priority on family time. Slow down your level of busyness and that of your family. Share some blackberries with them by an open fire tonight.

✢ ✢ ✢

17

The Power of an Encouraging Word

No matter how well things may be going for you right now, you could probably use some encouragement. You for sure could use some encouragement if things *aren't* going so well. The fact is that everyone needs encouragement. Sometimes we need it in small doses, like a pep talk from a dad, a kind word from a spouse or a verbal shot in the arm from a family member who helps get our thinking on the right track. Other times we need heavy dosages of encouragement to get us through a malaria of despair. Whatever the need or the amount, God has gifted human beings to be encouragers to one another while we're here on earth. Sure, we can receive heavenly encouragement from God, but sometimes we're like the little girl who woke up scared in the middle of the night and ran into her parents room. "Don't worry, honey," her parents soothed her. "God will protect you." "I know that," said the little girl. "But I needed some protection with skin on it!"

So people are God's encouragement with skin on. And I know of no more powerful way to give encouragement than through words. The writer of the Old Testament book of Proverbs says the tongue holds the power of life and death. We need to use this little appendage for something more than working on ice cream cones. We need to speak words of encouragement to others. Just a word or two, spoken at the right time, can make all the difference in how our day goes. It's particularly important that families pour on the encouragement because home is where we retreat from the harsh realities of the world. If we don't find encouragement at home, we're not likely to find it elsewhere.

But we can do more than simply speak words of encouragement. Written words are also powerful encouragers and carry with them an added benefit; they linger. The note of encouragement you write to a friend or family member can travel with him or her for a long time, be pulled out of a pocket or purse at any time, and continue to furnish the lift it did when it was originally received.

A few years ago someone close to my wife and me was going through a hard time in her marriage. She and her husband lived out of state, and we were frustrated by our inability to be by her side to encourage her. As an alternative we decided to write a letter. At first I thought it was a poor substitute to "being there" but later, after talking with our friend, she assured us she was reading the letter daily and drawing strength from it. I include it here, with our friend's permission, not because the letter itself is a work of art, but because the story in the letter is such a great encouragement—and because I believe it illustrates the powerful impact of our words:

Dearest Susan:

We're thinking of you so much these days and wanted to remind you of our thoughts and prayers by way of this note. We're sending along a news story that's meant a lot to us from the 1992 Olympics about a runner named Derek Redmond. As you can see from the story, Redmond had trained for a long time to run the 400 meters. But in the middle of the race he popped his right hamstring and suffered an excruciatingly painful injury. Rather than quitting the race, though, he kept hobbling, limping and falling, determined to finish even though it was clear his hopes for a medal had disappeared.

The part that we found so meaningful was about his dad's actions. After seeing his son hurt, he forgot all about "proper protocol" and pushed his way out of the stands, past security people to get out on the track to his son. Putting his arm around Derek he helped him around the track the rest of the way and then, at the finish line, let Derek cross on his own. Derek's official result in the race showed "no time" and race officials listed him as having "abandoned" the race but, as the paper says, that was far from the truth. Both Derek and his dad showed something not often seen these days—perseverance and support in the face of adversity.

And we've thought how much Derek's dad acted just like the Heavenly Father does when we go through adversity—just like He's doing with you. You've trained a long time and put hope, energy, time and commitment into your marriage just like Redmond did with his training. Now something's happened that makes it look like you won't be able to finish the race; excruciating pain that causes you to sob with hurt and disappointment. But you're still going, just like Derek. And just like Derek's dad, the Heavenly Father is coming out of the stands to be there with you. He's no longer a spectator but He's brushing past proper protocol and

*security guards to make His way to you on the track
where you're in despair and crying. With gentle, but
strong arms He's encircling you with His love, bidding
you to keep on, helping you as you shift your weight
onto Him. And at the right time, He'll release you to
take the last few steps on your own to cross the finish
line.*

*We know there aren't any pat, easy answers and simply
writing a letter about a courageous Olympic athlete is
an inadequate balm for your wounds. But be assured
of our Father's love that pushes Him out of the stands
and onto the track to carry you when you hurt. And be
equally assured of our constant love and affection for
you. We love you Susan.*

I'd like to say there was a happy ending to this story and the
marriage was restored. Unfortunately, my friend and her
husband divorced. But I'm confident the encouragement
Susan received, not only from us but from many friends
near and far away, helped sustain her through her hard times.

You can be an encourager too. Look for those opportunities to speak or write a word or letter of encouragement. It
doesn't have to be long. It doesn't have to be eloquent. It
just has to be sincere, a message sent from heart to heart,
timely, and targeted at a person in need. My most memorable notes of encouragement came as a child from my mom
and dad. Dad always left me a note under my cereal bowl
at the breakfast table, wishing me a good day before he
headed off to an early morning at the factory while I was
still asleep. Mom always put a note in my lunch bag (I was
the only kid who got a lunch with a commercial). Her

handwritten expression of love tided me over until I got home from school. The short, homespun notes of encouragement gave me a boost and reminded me someone cared, even when the world was beating me up.

You can do the same thing. Write a note of encouragement to someone right now. Maybe to your mom or dad, to your son or daughter, or maybe to that irritating little brother or that obnoxious older sister. Whomever you choose, send them a message of encouragement from the heart. It will help them continue the race and cross the finish line, knowing that they're not alone and that someone cares.

18

Talking & Listening Lessons for Men

This column is for guys. Women, you can turn the page and read about people who bowled 300 last night. I don't mean to be discriminatory, but this is "man-talk."

I want to talk with you men about a topic we all hate to hear about: communication. We've probably all been drilled by a girlfriend or wife about how we don't talk to them enough—or we don't tell them we love them enough—or we don't pay attention when they're talking. Does any of this sound familiar?

If it does you're not alone. Just a couple of weeks ago I received this letter from a female reader:

"Dear Jim—You recently wrote about loving your spouse in the way they need to be loved. I have tried to beat this into my husband's head forever. He feels that saying "I love you" too often takes away the significance of it, even though I am a person who needs to hear those words often. He feels loved through touch and is always wanting me to show him attention by putting my hand on his neck or leg, and if I fail to do so he feels neglected. Yet he cannot seem to see the same correlation with my need for hearing those three words."

This woman's complaint is shared by many. Let's face it guys, we are wired for communication in a different way, than women. Author Gary Smalley reported in his book, *Love is a Decision,* that the average woman speaks roughly

25,000 words a day, and the average man speaks only 12,500. Smalley says, "What this means is a woman is often left holding her cup out for meaningful conversation day after day and drawing it back with only a few drops to nourish her." We just don't use verbal conversation all that much. And when we do, it's often to give advice and "fix problems," instead of listening from the heart.

This came home to me loud and clear during a conversation I had with my wife several years ago. After pouring out her heart to me about some problem she was facing, I exclaimed in frustration, "What do you want me to do about it?" She looked dumbstruck. "I don't want you to *do* anything about it," she said. "I just want you to listen to me without offering advice." Oops. I forgot it's not my job to "fix" everything. Sometimes I'm just supposed to listen.

The most frequent reason men are held back from promotions at work is "lack of relationship skills." For whatever reason we just aren't naturally attentive to relationships. But women are more inclined that way and have a "built in relationship manual." Most women desire good healthy relationships and have a natural ability to recognize one. It seems sensible for us men to tap into this gold mine of relationship skill by asking our spouse or girlfriend three simple questions:

> 1) *On a scale of one to ten, with one being terrible and ten being great, where would you like our relationship to be?* Most people—men and women—will tell you they want their close personal relationships to be around a nine or ten.
>
> 2) *On a scale of one to ten, overall, where would you*

rate our relationship today? In most cases, Gary Smalley says, the man will rate the relationship two to three points higher than his wife or girlfriend. Don't be shocked by the answer of your partner, and whether you agree or not, give her your full attention as you ask question 3.

3) As you look at our relationship, what are some specific things we could do over the next six weeks that would move us closer to a ten? Most women will have specific ideas, but your wife or girlfriend may be reluctant to answer truthfully for fear of hurting your feelings. Be patient and let her speak the truth. Your relationship will definitely improve if you hear her out and begin implementing her suggestions.

Is there a benefit to all this "talking" stuff? You bet. Recent surveys of happily married couples reveal that the most common trait they shared was the willingness of the husband to listen to and take the advice of his wife. Looking for more benefits? Dr. James J. Lynch in his book, *The Language of the Heart,* sets forth compelling evidence that effective communication skills improve a person's cardiovascular health. Holding words and feelings inside is correlated with extremely high blood pressure. For our own health as well as the health of our relationships, we need to learn to talk and listen.

All of this does not come naturally to us men. But then again, neither did hitting a baseball or a golf ball the first time. But with patient persistence we finally learned how to do these things, and we can learn to effectively communicate with the women in our lives as well. Try it today. Tap into that "relationship manual" and learn the pathway to a relationship that hits a ten on a ten scale. ✞

19

Send a Thanksgiving Thank You Note

My mom always taught me that it was polite to send a thank you note to someone after they had done something especially nice for you. You know the drill–people come to your birthday party and give you a present (usually something a size too small or a duplicate of something you already have!) and Mom gets in her "you gotta write a thank you note" mood. After all the punch cups were put away and the wrapping paper was stashed in the trash, Mom would get down the box of thank you cards she kept in the corner cupboard of the kitchen. She'd put the cards on the table along with a pen, and without much more than a "Here you go," she'd set me in motion to write thank you notes to my birthday benefactors. I can't say I ever enjoyed writing those little notes, but I sure learned something from Mom. When someone does something nice for you, you have a moral obligation to thank them properly.

That's part of the motivation behind an annual Thanksgiving tradition at our house. When mid-November rolls around, our family takes inventory of our blessings. Over the dinner table we discuss different people who, over the course of the last year, have been a blessing in our lives–people for whom we're especially thankful as a family. Then we decide the person or family for whom we're most grateful, and we write them a letter, thanking them for who they are and what they've done in our lives. It doesn't take very long to come up with a good number of specific things these

folks have done over the last year. And once we've decided
on the person or family and compiled some specific items
they've done for us, we compose a Thanksgiving thank you
note telling them how much we appreciate their contribution to our lives. Is the whole thing a little corny? Probably.
Does it sound a little old fashioned? Undoubtedly. But
have we ever received a letter back from these folks declin-
ing the honor of being selected for the annual Thanksgiving letter? Not a chance!

Another part of the tradition is pulling out the file marked
"Thanksgiving letters" and leafing through the letters of past
years. We're reminded of those who have befriended us and
how God has blessed us in different ways, through different
people over the course of our lives. We find letters to an
elderly couple who made us feel at home when we first moved
to town, a middle aged couple who now live in Minnesota,
but were, at one time, precious neighbors down the street.
We find a youth minister, a children's choir director, and a
couple of letters to grandparents—a cornucopia of blessings in a growing manila file folder. It's impossible to just
put this year's letter inside and then close the file drawer. I
have to re-read each letter and re-live each year. Here's what
the letter looked like in 1989:

Dear Don and Leanne,

*We have a Thanksgiving tradition at our house. Each
Thanksgiving we write a letter to some person or family that we've been thankful for over the past year. We
talk about it as a family and try to decide on someone
who has been special to all of us. This year our family
decided you two were the special people!*

In the few short years we've known you in our neighborhood, we couldn't help but be impressed with your selfless, giving spirit. Your willingness to host volleyball games, Halloween parties, Neighborhood Association meetings, and your gracious hospitality are clear indications of your caring attitude. But it's also clear that your willingness to help springs from a heart that seeks to serve others, and it's the inner motivation even more than the outward action that touched us this year.

Your quick smiles, friendly waves and genuine interest in us let us know we were more than just fellow residents on the same street. We were "neighbors" in the old-fashioned sense of the word. Even my children could feel your warmth, as evidenced by their frequent requests to "take a walk down the street to Don and Leanne's house." You just can't beat a child's perceptiveness.

For all the Association work, for the times you plowed snow from our driveway, for letting us borrow tools, for watching our kids and sharing our laughter, and for just being you, we wanted to say a heartfelt thanks. We count it an honor and privilege to have shared our street, our lives and this year with you.

Have a happy Thanksgiving.

Don and Leanne really appreciated our letter that year. Why, we even got a thank you card from them for our thank you card to them. This thankfulness thing got downright contagious!

The tradition lives on at our house—and it could at your house as well. Isn't there someone your family could write a thank you note to this Thanksgiving? Maybe it's a favorite baby sitter, or a pastor, rabbi or priest, a neighbor, a relative, or someone in the public arena whom you have appreciated from afar. It doesn't take much time (about 20 minutes) or money (about 32 cents) to drop a Thanksgiving thank you note in the mail. Just open up that corner cabinet in the kitchen and get your box of cards and pen out. Gather everyone around and vote on the candidates. Then write your Thanksgiving thank you note. You'll be glad you did, and so will that someone whose address appears on the envelope.

✛ ✛ ✛

20

Reaping What You Sow

Old Mr. Silverstein was our back neighbor. He was usually a very pleasant gentleman with thinning, grey hair and a friendly wave and smile. I most often saw him with a rake or a hoe in his hand, tending his garden. His voice would boom across the chest high wire fence, "Hellooooo Jimmy! How's that garden coming?" I was about ten-years-old, and he was probably in his 60s, and we were both "city farmers" trying to grow authentic vegetables in our small squares of turned dirt between close-by houses.

Mr. Silverstein's garden always did better than mine. He had more time to tend it. He was more methodical in his weeding and fertilizing. He always prided himself on having the first red, ripe tomato in the neighborhood. My garden was puny by comparison–a few cukes, a sprinkling of lettuce, hidden carrots growing silently beneath the soil, and of course the tomatoes. Mr. Silverstein and I always had a tomato race to see who would have the first ripe tomato. He always won.

My mother had encouraged me to plant a garden. She grew up on the farm and always seemed to have some special kinship with the earth. She would often come out to "inspect" my garden and offer some very gentle suggestions. She smiled approvingly at the frail fence I constructed to keep my beagle, Skipper, from digging up the seedlings. And she was an active encourager in the annual race for the first red tomato—getting me started early and occasionally pulling some weeds. As with all moms, she wanted to see her son's tomato plants "win."

But it seems we never did. Mr. Silverstein's green thumb was always the first to stick up in the air announcing victory. Year after year my spindly tomato plants, tied like hostages to a wooden stake, would apologetically lag behind. Until one year. That was the year my mother (always the practical joker) decided to take the tomato race into her own hands.

One night, after dark, Mom snuck out to the garden. With flashlight in hand, she tied an artificial, plastic, red tomato to one of our plants. Then she stole quietly back into the house giggling like a school girl.

The next morning, like clockwork, Mr. Silverstein walked out to his garden, hoe in hand. We watched from our side of the fence as he stood, gape-jawed, staring at the red orb dangling from my otherwise unimpressive plant. He sputtered and fussed incomplete sentences—something about, "I don't remember seeing that before...how could it...I don't believe it..." and stomped up and down the fence line. My mother and I could not control our laughter and, in reluctant honesty, confessed our sin. Funny. Mr. Silverstein didn't think it was all that humorous. I guess he took his garden pretty seriously.

I'm glad my mom urged me to plant a garden. I'm glad she didn't think it had to be perfect. I'm glad she helped me know the taste of fresh tomatoes, carrots, lettuce and cucumbers, even if they were kind of scrawny and would never appear on the Miracle-Gro® commercials. From planting my garden I learned, like the farmers, about depending on God's providence in the weather. I worried, like the farmers, about too little or too much rain. I sowed in hope, weeded in sweat, and harvested in joy—all on a very small scale. But it was an experience that gave me a little hint about a different way of life outside city bounds. Thanks to Mom, I also learned about having a little fun along the way—even if it was at the temporary expense of Mr. Silverstein.

This year, for the first time in a long time, I planted some tomato plants. Like my plants of old, they're not doing too well. I'm not especially faithful about weeding or watering or fertilizing. But when my son Spence and I planted them, we were "honorary farmers for a day." It felt good to get dirt under our nails, to pause for a cold drink in the shade of a tree and survey our "plowing." And maybe, just maybe, we'll have a ripe, red tomato hanging on one of those limp little plants before too long.

Our families are like a garden. They take the careful cultivation of relationships. They need the refreshing water of encouragement. They demand the weeding out of too many activities. They require some "fencing off" of bad influences. Your garden/family, like mine, may not be perfect, but you can gain real satisfaction from working at the process. You don't have to "compete" with your neighbor—just stay faithful in working at your family garden every day. And along the way, have fun. You can enjoy the fruits—or the vegetables—of your labor for years to come.

21

Quality Time or Quantity Time

A national magazine carried this testimonial from a young, successful attorney:

> "The greatest gift I ever received was a gift I got one Christmas when my dad gave me a small box. Inside was a note saying, 'Son, this year I will give you 365 hours—an hour every day after dinner. It's yours. We'll talk about what you want to talk about, we'll go where you want to go, play what you want to play. It will be your hour.' My dad not only kept his promise that year, but every year he renewed it. That was the greatest gift I ever had in my life. I am the result of his time."

I don't know if you've ever received a gift like that, or if you've ever given a gift like that, but it's the kind of gift I'd love to get and to give. Although my dad and mom didn't wrap up a box with a note inside, they did spend time investing in my life and the life of my sister. My dad spent countless hours playing catch with me in the backyard. Only later did I learn that Dad never played ball as a boy and learned along with me. He even had to go out and find a left-handed mitt! But he took the time to drag his work-wearied body out back every night and help me learn not to be afraid of the ball.

Mom did the same kind of investing. Many a night she

would pour over homework assignments with me, helping me memorize obscure facts or geographic names by putting them to music or making up a silly rhyme. If I ever snickered at her wacky, creative approach to scholastic achievement she'd gently scold me, "You may laugh now, but you'll be glad for this silly rhyme when you take your test." And I always was.

The time my folks spent with me was never segregated into "quality" or "quantity" time. It was just time. They didn't spend it with me because they had to, or because they felt guilty, or because some parenting book told them to. They spent time with me because they knew I needed it. They did it because they inherently knew it was the right thing to do. Granted, it wasn't time spent analyzing our relationship or engaging in deep philosophical or spiritual discussions. It was just moments spent together, and our relationship grew more because of the unhurried expenditure of time in each other's presence.

We need to just spend more time together in our families. Unhurried, stick-whittling, rock-kicking, cloud-staring time together. It doesn't have to be organized. It doesn't have to be orchestrated. It doesn't have to be done the way some parental advice book says it should be. If we'll just weave our children into the warp and woof of our lives, we'll begin to knit together an intimate family.

No agenda. No time frame. No topic for discussion. Just being together with those we love. It may be sitting on the front porch together–laying in the grass staring at the stars–walking through Martin Nature Center on an ambling sort of hike. It might even be doing chores or taking a car ride together.

I have come to believe that more effective communication can take place between a father and a son over the hood of a car engine than can be accomplished sitting face-to-face in awkward conversation. I think it's infinitely easier for a mom to talk to a teen when they're both looking out the windshield of a car, taking a drive, than when they engage in formal discussion. It's like that old saying, "Life is what happens to you when you're preparing for something else." Relationships are deepened between parent and child during the least noticed moments of life.

Build into your schedule some "unplanned" time. Don't cram your days so full of activities that there's no space for "quantity" time. Don't let your calendar or DayTimer® run your relationships. Quality time is important. But you have a better chance of getting true quality time the more quantity time you spend with your children.

✜ ✜ ✜

22

Learning When to Shut Up

One day when I was about ten-years-old, I found myself in a school yard fist fight with a guy older, stronger and tougher than me. It wasn't a pretty result. After a miserable display of my lack of boxing skills, I sat down on the curb to lick my wounds and cry a little. Just then, another kid walked by and started to make fun of me. "Got beat up huh, Priest, you little wimp!" Ever quick with my lips I shot back, "Shut up or I'll punch you out." Unfortunately the other kid decided to find out if I could—and after a few minutes in the ring with my second boxing partner I found out I couldn't. This kid even broke one of my teeth. I was humiliated—two embarrassing defeats in the same morning on the same playground. When I got home that night and told my pa what happened he said, "Son, you're either going to have to learn to fight, or you're going to have to learn to keep your mouth shut." I had several more fights—and defeats—before I finally learned the truth of what Pa had to say. Opening your mouth at the wrong time and in the wrong way can get you beat up—in more ways than one.

Take the dad who loves to needle family members. He really doesn't mean any harm, but he just can't help showing what a witty guy he is by putting others down. Does he ever develop intimate relationships with his kids? Does his behavior generate feelings of loyalty and respect? Or how about the sister who can't keep a secret? Things you told her "in confidence" are barely off your lips before the verbal e-mail has gone out, and the whole block knows about your confidential conversation. Even well-meaning family members can betray a confidence by telling private matters to others in an effort to "keep them informed" or so they can "pray about the situation." Let's face it: most of us talk way too much, and when we do speak, it's often about the wrong things.

The New Testament book of James tells us that the task of conquering the tongue is a tough one. "No one can tame the tongue," James says. "It is a restless evil and full of deadly poison" (James 3:8). James compares the tongue to a little flame that sets a whole forest on fire—its potential for destruction is tremendous. But James also talks about its positive attributes, likening it to a rudder that directs a ship and a bridle in a horse's mouth. He tells us the tongue issues curses, but can also issue blessings. Here in Oklahoma we'd say the tongue is a bucking broncho without a saddle—it's tough to tame but if you can get it busted, you'd have yourself a good horse. The tongue can be a great thing for building up people, for encouraging, for motivating, or for making folks laugh. The problem is knowing when to shut it off. Too often the tongue is like the Duracell® battery rabbit—it just keeps going and going. So here are some quick ideas for learning how to shut up (and then I'll be quiet).

Avoid sarcasm in the family. For some folks this may be a Herculean effort. Consciously decide not to make fun of other family members or make demeaning remarks about them. Remember the Greek root for the word "sarcasm" means to cut ("casm") the flesh ("sarc"), so when you cut somebody down, you're literally cutting their flesh. Don't cut up your family with your tongue.

Listen more to others and talk less about yourself. A young lady went out one evening with the British statesman Benjamin Disraeli and had dinner the next evening with his rival, politician William Gladstone. When asked to compare the two famous men she said, "When I was with Mr. Disraeli, I thought *he* was the wittiest man on earth. But when I was with Mr. Gladstone, I thought *I* was the wittiest girl on earth." You want to leave family members thinking about how good they feel about themselves, not how good you feel about yourself.

Be absolutely reliable in keeping a confidence. If a family member entrusts a secret to you, don't share it—period. Don't ask anyone to pray about it with you unless you have the confidant's permission. In other words, keep a secret a secret with all the vigor and integrity that you keep your own secrets secret.

It's never too late to shut up. If you start saying something you shouldn't, clam up. If you begin breaching a confidence, silence yourself. Even if it's embarrassing just stop talking. Don't tell yourself, "Well, I've already started to say this so the cat's out of the bag." Instead, stick the cat back in the bag and zip it.

If you'll follow these suggestions and control your tongue you might save some bumps and bruises—to yourself and your family. And now I'll shut up.

23

Juggling for the Family Klutz

A friend once gave me a book called *Juggling for the Complete Klutz*. I thought the title was amusing rather than an insulting but accurate description of myself. However, my amusement only lasted until I used the book to teach myself how to juggle. I failed. I just couldn't seem to keep all the balls in the air at one time. Even with a step by step, simple description (with pictures!) I out-klutzed the complete klutz. How humiliating!

Some of us feel that same way about trying to juggle all our family responsibilities. We try desperately to keep all the balls in the air—run the kids to activities, keep up with household chores, be involved in civic groups, attend church, maintain a job and—oh yes—occasionally take some time for ourselves. But like a laughable clown in the circus who can't learn how to juggle, we find there are more things to juggle than we have hands or time. How then do we keep all the balls in the air? Here's some advice from one klutz who has trouble juggling but keeps on trying:

Recognize you're human. Many of us have high expectations of ourselves and think we should be Superdad or Supermom, able to leap tall loads of laundry in a single bound! But face it—we simply can't get everything done that cries out for attention. We have a finite amount of time and energy and, like it or not, the list of responsibilities for today's family is most definitely not finite! So go a bit easier on yourself. Admit you may have bitten off more than you can chew.

Don't mentally spank yourself for your failures to keep up with it all. Instead, when guilt comes calling, chase it away with some reassuring self talk like, "Hey, I'm doing the best I can," "There are a lot of other folks who are in the same predicament I'm in," or "For someone as feeble, old and decrepit as I am I'm doing pretty well!" Seriously, we need to recognize that we live in a demanding age and we are not incompetent or inadequate simply because we feel over-whelmed.

Streamline your life. After you've admitted you can't get everything done that is crying out for attention, do what you can to streamline things. This is especially helpful during times of crisis and time crunches. Focus only on the things that are truly important, that must be done, and that must be done in the very near future. While I am a firm believer in carrying through on commitments, we have to teach ourselves how to say "no" every once in a while and when to jettison unnecessary involvements. Under the old 80/20 principle, 20% of the people do 80% of the work in any group. So if you're in the 20%, lighten up on your commitments (and if you're in the 80% start carrying your fair share!). But remember to streamline. Eliminate the unnecessary, whether it be clutter in your house, involvements with outside groups, or activities for your children. Begin teaching your children the art of simplicity by limiting the number of involvements they have. It will provide more time for them and for you and will result in a less hectic home life.

Organize yourself. Some Type A personality folks are naturally organized, but there are some of us Type B personalities that hate making lists and go out of our way to avoid that dreadful, fun-dampening disease called organization. But whether you are inclined to organize yourself or not there is magic in the "o-word." Things tend to run more smoothly, life is less hazardous and wild and, amazingly, you can get more accomplished in less time. Think about ways you can organize your house, your life and your family. Delegate jobs to other family members. Teach your children about assuming responsibility for household chores on a regular basis and organize the time and manner in which they are to get the chores done. Adopt some routines for yourself as well, whether it involves chores, relaxation time or family activities. Getting organized is a key step to successful juggling.

Prioritize. In *The Seven Habits of Highly Effective People,* Stephen Covey talks about putting "first things first," and that simple piece of advice is one of the most important habits of a happy juggler. We must recognize that not all people or projects in our lives are equal. Some demand and merit more attention than others. We must learn who these people and projects are and not let less significant people or projects drain our time and energy. This requires us to assess ourselves, our commitments, and our goals for ourselves and our families. Florence Nightingale said, "Since I was twenty-four there never was any vagueness as to what God's work was for me." We need to remove the vagueness in our lives as well and prioritize our time and involvements in order to keep those important balls in the air.

Four simple steps for juggling family responsibilities. Even a complete klutz could handle these! Why not adopt these practical points and amaze your friends and family with your juggling ability! ✢

24

Life is Like Home-Made Ice Cream

I feel real sorry for my children. In fact, my sadness extends to most of the young people born in recent years. Nearly all of the young people I know are deprived. It's a shame. But unfortunately, that's the America we now live in. Widespread deprivation among children.

And my kids are just like the rest. Deprived. What's worse, they don't even know how deprived they are. How are they —and thousands of other young people in America—sorely deprived? They have never known the pleasure of hand-cranking their own ice cream in the summer time.

In the days before ice cream vendors were popping up on every street corner with 31 varieties, folks made their own ice cream at home. They didn't make it in those "real imitation wood-simulated" electric ice cream machines that Service Merchandise sells. Ice cream used to be made in tall metal containers with a smaller metal container inside. For those of you who have forgotten (or never knew), here's how the process worked:

First you fill the small, inner container with the ingredients for the ice cream. Milk, sugar, vanilla, whipping cream, strawberries and probably some other stuff I've forgotten. Next you place the lid on the small container. This small lid has wooden paddles that go down into the gooey mixture. The real, homemade ice cream connoisseur knows this paddle device is called the "dasher." Once you place the lid on the smaller container you place the whole thing inside the big container, leaving a gap of about two inches all around between the smaller and larger container. In that gap you put crushed ice, crammed down tight, and then sprinkled intermittently and liberally with rock salt to make the ice melt and help harden the ice cream. Another lid is placed on the larger container, and this second lid has a hand-crank that will turn the dasher inside the small container. (Isn't this fascinating?) The crank is then turned vigorously for what seems like several hours (but is really only about 20 minutes) until the dasher won't turn easily. This means the ice cream has pretty well hardened. Then comes the most agonizing part—you remove the dasher, wrap the entire thing in towels, and wait for the ice cream to harden just right. I always hated the waiting part! The whole process takes an hour from start to finish, but the waiting part seemed like it took days. But throughout the experience you enjoy a good workout on your arm, fun conversation around the ice cream maker, and a wonderful kind of anticipation that cannot be found waiting in line at Baskin Robbins®.

I remember the ache of my arm, the gnawing of my stomach and the coolness of the melting mixture sliding down my throat. Our old ice cream maker had a leak in the small container so there was always a hint of the flavor of rock salt in our ice cream. Never mind. It tasted great on a hot summer day.

As I recollect those times, I'm sad my own children have never experienced them. As I said, they're deprived. But at least I can tell them about those days, and tell them how life is a little bit like hand-cranked ice cream.

You get out of life what you put in—like the ingredients in hand-cranked ice cream.

You don't get anything out of life without work—like hand-cranking until your arm hurts.

Sometimes you have to do things to help the process along—like adding rock salt to melt the ice or wrapping the towel around the container afterward.

Life doesn't always turn out perfect but don't worry, just enjoy it—like getting a little rock salt flavor in your ice cream.

The result is worth the effort—like sliding strawberry ice cream down your parched throat after working hard to create it in the back yard.

I think I'll just go buy myself an old-fashioned, hand-crank, ice cream machine and show my kids how to use it. I know it's not the easiest way to get ice cream. It's not the most convenient. It's sure not the fastest. But I'm convinced it's the best. Those who eat homemade, hand-cranked ice cream can never say they've been deprived. And I don't want my children to be deprived.

Marriage

family talk

25

Marriage Means Burning the Ships

When Spanish explorer Hernando DeSoto's ships reached the new world in the early 1500s, his crew was overjoyed at finally reaching their destination. But shortly after setting foot on shore, DeSoto gave a strange and discomforting command: "Burn the ships!" The men were dumbstruck. "But why?" they cried. "Because you are home now. There will be no turning back," replied DeSoto. So the ships were burned, and the men were given the supreme motivation to survive in the new land. They had to work together. There was no turning back.

DeSoto's story of total commitment should be required as part of all marriage ceremonies. When a man and a woman marry, both should "burn the ships," and with DeSoto-like resolve work together to survive—and thrive—in their "new world." What ships should be burned by every newlywed?

The first ship is dependence on parents. The newlywed's spouse must take first status in their heart and their life. I am certainly not advocating an abandonment of mother and father, but the Bible counsels, "For this reason a man shall *leave* his mother and father and *cleave* to his wife." Both the "leaving" and the "cleaving" are important elements of a healthy marriage. Continued dependence on Mom and Dad after the marriage can have a disabling effect on a newlywed. So when you marry, you must close an era with your parents to begin a new one with your spouse. Even though it's sometimes hard to do, you must swear first allegiance to your spouse.

A second ship that must be burned is "old flames." Too many young marrieds think they can still maintain a close relationship with their old girlfriend or boyfriend and not have it affect their marriage. While there may be exceptions to the rule, the general principle still holds—a lingering romance or smoldering relationship can spell ruin for a new marriage. It may be painful and it may seem extreme, but wisdom dictates that old romances be ended when you head for the marriage altar. Don't keep phoning or writing or meeting your "old flame" after you marry. If you do, you're literally flirting with trouble.

A third ship to burn is the one called divorce. Too many marriages are entered into with this thought in the back of the mind: "If our marriage doesn't work out, we can always get a divorce." This kind of thinking has given rise to the dismal statistic that one out of every two marriages in America ends in divorce. Divorce cannot be entertained as an option if you want your marriage to survive. Every couple encounters rough waters as they navigate through the sea of matrimony. Sometimes the ship is tossed about, takes on water, and looks to be swamped. That's when extra effort is needed to bail water—not abandon ship. Ban the word "divorce" from your marriage vocabulary. Don't use it as a weapon during an argument with your spouse or as an ultimatum when you're angry. Tell your spouse and your children, "We will never get divorced." Just saying the words aloud will increase your resolve to shun divorce and work hard at your marriage. It may not be easy to say. You may want to build in a loop hole or two—but don't do it. Make the unequivocal, unqualified promise "we will never get di-vorced" and then stick to it.

I sat across from a young person recently who was experi-encing marital problems. This person asked me, "Why would I want to hang around in a marriage that's not fun anymore?" I looked straight into their eyes and said, "Be-cause you made a promise in front of God and many wit-nesses that you would love and honor your spouse until death parted you." Ouch. Not a fun thought. But the marriage vow is a solemn oath that doesn't include any foot-notes or exceptions. We must honor our marital promise even when it's not "fun."

DeSoto's command wasn't a popular one, but it was effec-tive. It was the necessary motivation for his men to be to-tally committed to their new world. You'll probably feel some of the same things when you burn your ships upon entering marriage. It won't seem popular, but it does result in total commitment. And isn't that what our marriages really need? So burn the ships of parental dependence, old romances and divorce options! Work hard at surviving in—and enjoying—the "new world" of marriage.

26

The Gift of Sacrifice

The magical Christmas story called *The Gift of the Magi*, by O. Henry, has always captured the essence of the season for me. It's the story of a young, married couple—Jim and Della Young—who live a hand-to-mouth existence with little money to spend on Christmas presents. But they each have one prized personal possession of which they are supremely proud. Henry describes them this way:

> *Now there were two possessions of the James Dillingham Youngs in which they both took a mighty pride. One was Jim's gold watch that had been his father's and his grandfather's. The other was Della's hair. Had the Queen of Sheba lived in the flat across the airshaft, Della would have let her hair hang out the window some days to dry just to depreciate Her Majesty's jewels and gifts. Had King Solomon been the janitor, with all his treasures piled up in the basement, Jim would have pulled out his watch every time he passed, just to see him pluck at his beard from envy.*

As the short story unfolds we learn Della has no money to buy the perfect gift for Jim—a very expensive platinum watch fob. So she makes the supreme sacrifice. She cuts off and sells her beautiful, precious hair and uses the money to buy the chain for Jim to attach to his watch. She is giddy with excitement at the prospect of giving her Jim this wonderful gift, despite its personal cost to her.

When Jim sees what Della has done, he is stunned and stares in disbelief. He appreciates the gift more than he can say, but there is a wonderous twist of irony in it. You see, unknown to Della, he has sold his watch to buy her the tortoise shell combs Della had longed after in a shop window. Jim, like Della, had gladly given up his prized possession to purchase the perfect gift for his beloved. Now, Jim had a beautiful fob—but no watch, and Della had gorgeous hair combs—but no hair. Henry sums up the scene this way:

> *The magi, as you know, were wise men—wonderfully wise men—who brought gifts to the Babe in the manger. They invented the art of giving Christmas presents. And here I have lamely related to you the uneventful chronicle of two foolish children who most unwisely sacrificed for each other the greatest treasures of their house. But in the last word to the wise of these days let it be said that of all who give gifts these two were the wisest. Of all who give and receive gifts, such as they are wisest. Everywhere they are wisest. They are the magi.*

The gift of sacrifice is the best gift to give during this season. Not the expensive toys, the chic clothes, the stunning jewels or baubles that catch our eye. It is the gift of sacrifice that says to your recipient, "I love you and give you an important part of myself." Such gift giving takes forethought and insight; you cannot do it in a rush through the mall. This kind of gift giving takes a giving of ourselves.

You can give this gift to your family this season by trying some of these ideas:

Give "coupons" to your loved one—redeemable for a back rub, a home cooked meal, a "night out from the kids" or a "chore of your choice."

Bake a gift and hand wrap it in homemade paper. Even if you don't consider yourself a "chef," just take your best shot at it and add some personal creative flair.

Write your own card rather than buying one in the store. So you're not likely to rival Hallmark® for prettiness or rhyme—who cares? Just make it personal and your loved one will appreciate it more and longer than the store-bought kind.

Get out in the workshop and make something out of wood or paper or yarn or plaster. Visit a hobby center and find a craft you can do yourself.

These are just a few of the "homemade" gift ideas that could be given this season. With a little love and time and creativity you too can be one of the magi.

27

Don't Be So Sure
You're Right

I remember that blistering hot day twenty years ago in Electra, Texas when my wife and I said our wedding vows. After promising to love and cherish till death parted us, we headed off in Diane's very old Dodge. We weren't exactly sure how many miles it had left, but we knew it was on the edge. Nevertheless we decided to live on the edge ourselves and drive it cross country to our new home in Upstate New York.

The Dodge only made it as far as Oklahoma City before the transmission completely went out. The next day the car mechanic pronounced it economically irreparable, and we were left to purchase a new car on the third day of our young married lives. Fortunately the Lord had mercy on us, and we were able to purchase reliable transportation before what was left of our honeymoon was completely spoiled.

Driving along the next day, recounting our car tragedy, Diane remarked "I'm really going to miss that old Dart." I nodded and smiled a knowing, correcting smile, "Yes dear, but it wasn't a Dart, it was a Polaris." Now it was Diane's turn to smile knowingly. "Honey, I drove that car for five years, and I know it was a Dart." With a bit of an edge to my voice I increased my intensity and said, "My love, I know all about cars. Darts are small and your car was big, and it was most definitely a Polaris!"

Soon we were into the first official fight of our marriage. Neither of us could be wrong, of course. And the other one couldn't possibly be right. We dug in. We lobbed verbal grenades while we drove on in our hot, unairconditioned car with the black vinyl seats. The sun was sweltering, but the car wasn't the only thing getting hot. I wondered how she could be so dense. She was flabbergasted that I could be so stubborn. Finally we sank into an uncomfortable silence that went on for miles.

When we finally arrived at our destination that night I flopped onto the motel bed while Diane hit the shower. Pretty soon she emerged from the bathroom with a rather sheepish look on her face. "Good!" I thought to myself. "She's finally realized I was right about the car." Then she said those immortal words I'll never forget.

"You know, honey, I was wrong about the Dodge." There!! I knew it! I was vindicated! I began to silently gloat, but she cut me off. "And you were wrong too. Don't you remember, my car was a Dodge Coronet. We used to call it Cora Coronet!"

I got one of those embarrassed "oops" looks on my face and immediately regretted my hasty jumping to conclusions. She was right. It *was* a Coronet. We both apologized and had a good laugh over our mutual ignorance. And we learned a valuable rule in marital argumentation and debate. Don't be so sure you're right even when you're sure you're right.

While we were driving that day, if you had asked Diane if she could possibly have been wrong she would have vigorously denied it. I would have done the same. We were both obstinately committed to our own erroneous truth. And we got into an unpleasant disagreement because of our stubbornness.

These days whenever my wife and I have a disagreement, we try to remember the Coronet. We're not perfect about doing that and we still lapse into episodes of "I'm right and you're wrong." But when we remember the Coronet it causes us to stop. To re-evaluate our position. To recognize we might be wrong. To carefully listen to the other side. Our "first week of marriage" learning lesson was one we've had to re-learn many times, but because we had that first argument we've been able to do a better job in resolving other disagreements over the years.

The next time you find yourself in a heated disagreement with your marriage partner, remember the Coronet. You may be absolutely sure you're right. You may be totally convinced your spouse is wrong. But in a world where we have imperfect memories and limited knowledge, it's always good to recognize there's at least a chance you could be wrong. On our drive down the road of life it's a lesson worth remembering.

‡ ‡ ‡

28

Working on Your Marriage by Yourself

Susan didn't want a divorce. Ken said he didn't really want one either but, in his mind, their marriage "just wasn't working out." The spark was gone. They argued more than they kissed. He felt "suffocated and trapped." No, he didn't want to go to counseling—that was soft fluff that did no good and cost money. "I'm just going to move out and let's try to be friends," Ken said. So methodically they sat down at the kitchen table with pencil and paper and tried to make their limited income support two separate household budgets. Meanwhile, their three-year-old played in the living room, oblivious to the destruction taking place in the next room.

This scene is repeated, with minor variations, hundreds of times a week. One spouse decides to throw in the marital towel despite an earnest vow they took years earlier to "love and cherish 'till death parts us." Sometimes the couple gets divorced. Sometimes they just live apart. Sometimes they continue to share the same household but share little else. What can a person do when their spouse has given up on the marriage?

Dr. Ed Wheat, in his short but very helpful book "How to Save Your Marriage Alone," offers some suggestions:

Don't give up. Marriage counselor Anne Kristin Carrols says, "If you think there's no hope because you are the only one in your relationship who wants or cares enough to try to save your marriage, you are wrong! In my experience, most torn marriages are brought to new life, new vitality, by the interest of only one party." Dr. Wheat says the outcome of a troubled marriage depends, in the great majority of cases, on one committed partner's ability to behave consistently in accord with biblical principles designed by the Author of marriage. So don't give up hope.

Clarify your thoughts. The "innocent" spouse will be whipped about by the winds of outsider advice. Some will urge divorce. Some will recommend retribution. But the Author of marriage never counsels these things. "What God has joined together let no man put asunder" (Matthew 19:4-6). Dr. Wheat urges a "total mental commitment" to making your marriage work. Otherwise you'll be "swamped by waves of human opinion and bad advice." Determine in your mind that your course of action will be one of commitment to the marriage.

Stabilize your emotions. In a magazine article entitled "Fly by the Instruments," Gloria Okes Perkins writes that times of trials and emotional instability are like times of fog and air turbulence when piloting a plane. You can't see well. You're scared. You feel lost. That's the time the pilot must rely on the instruments, those unchanging guides. Likewise, during troubled times undisciplined feelings can cause a crash unless a person keeps stabilized on something unchangeable—like the Word of God. You can fly through fog and you can pilot your way through emotional turbulence only by relying on the right guidance system and not allowing emotions to take over. Fly your life-plane based on the unchanging guidance of God's Word, and don't make

99

emotion-based, reactive choices.

Learn how to love your partner. Someone in the marriage has to take the initiative to love their partner. That will seem impossible. They've hurt you. They've cheated on you. They don't deserve to be loved. But in order to breathe life back into your marriage you must take the initiative. You may need to love the person "by faith" at first. This means acting in a loving way even when you don't feel like it. As Dr. Wheat says, "Is it possible in your own marriage, that two lonely people are crying out for love on the inside, yet confused about what the other really wants and feels? There is only one constructive answer. You must choose to love your partner unilaterally at first and do it by meeting not only his or her needs but their desires as well." Determine what makes your spouse feel loved and try to show affection toward them by displaying love that way. Don't love them the way *you* want to love them, love them the way *they* need to be loved.

It's true that it will seem phony. It's true you won't feel like doing it. It's true the other person doesn't deserve it. But Dr. Wheat is convinced it works, and stories from his counseling practice confirm it. At least it's worth a try.

I recognize that simple sounding answers and words of advice in a newspaper column only go so far. They are like Bactine® antiseptic spray on an amputated limb. But they are offered with a hope and a prayer that some reader, about to give up on a seemingly doomed relationship, will be encouraged to continue working on their marriage even if they have to work on it alone. ✢

29

Love Notes

Through most of my school days, even through my first year in law school, my mom always packed me a brown bag lunch. This was no mere "sandwich in a bag" however. My mom always included several courses and sometimes even packed a tossed salad in a wide mouth thermos (salad dressing not included). Believe me, there was no lunch to compare with a Marge Priest packed lunch.

But of all the things Mom packed in my lunch the thing I liked the best were her love notes. I can't remember ever getting a lunch that didn't have some little scrap of paper in it with my mom's quickly penned sentiment. Sometimes it was just "Love ya! Mom." Other times she'd tell me she was proud of me, or I looked nice that morning or to have a great day. I was the only kid I knew who got a commercial in his lunch. But it was a tangible affirmation of my mom's love.

My dad did something similar. Most mornings my dad would get up early and be gone to work by the time I rolled out of bed. I'd sleepily make my way down to the breakfast table which had been set the night before and there, under my cereal bowl, my dad usually left me a note to get my day off on the right foot. His notes were short—like Mom's—and they were usually just a quick confirmation of his love. But I looked forward to lifting up the edge of the cereal bowl every morning to find an expression of affection from my dad.

I'm afraid I don't do as well as my parents in the love-note-writing department. I've got lots of good excuses. My kids don't take a brown bag lunch. I'm usually around in the mornings at breakfast to personally wish them a good day. But these excuses all seem to fall a little flat. So as often as I can remember, I try to leave little love notes to my loved ones. There's something just a little more tangible and lingering about a love note.

I like love notes because you can carry them around with you and look at them later. Spoken words of love are good and necessary, but they're like vapor. Once spoken they may abide in the ear for awhile, but they can't be unfolded in the hand and re-read. That's why I want to write more love notes. I don't expect my family to keep them in an album or anything. They may not even stuff them in their pocket to look at later. But a note in the hand is worth two in the bush. And it communicates fond affection in a very real way.

I'm also going to write more love notes to my wife. I've noticed she's still carrying around the last one I wrote about a year ago. It was just a little post-it note I stuck on the check register she carries in her purse. Something for her to find in an unexpected moment when I wasn't around. I've noticed its corners are getting tattered and the stickiness is about worn off. But it clings tenaciously to its spot in her purse—a constant reminder to her that she's the one for me.

In junior high love notes were a hot commodity. They were folded into funny triangles and passed, secret-agent like, around the room when the teacher wasn't looking. Then

we graduated into high school, and we all got too sophisti-
cated to write love notes, didn't we? Maybe we were on to
something in junior high that we shouldn't have lost. Maybe
we need to write more love notes to the ones we love.

How about today? Put the paper down right now. Find a
scrap of paper and a pen. Don't worry about it looking
fancy. Don't be concerned that it isn't poetic. Just scribble
out a few heartfelt lines and stick the note where your loved
one will find it later. In a pocket. In a drawer. In a shoe. In
a wallet. Maybe even in a brown bag lunch or under a
cereal bowl.

I'm betting that if you write love notes often enough your
loved ones will talk about it for years to come.

✝ ✝ ✝

30

Hitting the Mark on Valentine's Day

Greg and Janice had a good relationship—except around the "horrible holidays" (as Greg called them). Inevitably, it seemed, the day before or the day of their anniversary, or Valentine's Day, or some other special occasion they'd end up in some kind of fight and have a miserable "celebration." Greg finally concluded that it was the "anniversary effect"— some mystical bad aura which conspired to undermine their marriage seemed to surround those special days. Actually, the problem was a bit simpler and less mystical: lack of communication. The problem was that Greg wasn't taking these special days seriously enough, and Janice felt this meant Greg didn't really love her. They finally beat the "anniversary effect" by Janice telling Greg what it was she wanted to do on that special day and Greg taking the initiative to do some advance planning for the event.

Admit it guys. We don't always think ahead about making those special days special. Whether it's an anniversary or Valentine's Day, the ladies seem to do a better job, overall, at anticipating these things. We of the male persuasion seem to be on "full stun" when we realize in the early morning hours of February 14 that "today's the day I forgot to remember." So in the interest of achieving or preserving family unity I thought I'd pass along some test-driven ideas for making Valentine's Day (or any special occasion) something other than a space maintainer between days on the calendar.

Go to the store a week ahead and buy three or four appropriate greeting cards. They don't have to be expensive. Mix 'em up—some funny, some serious, maybe even a homemade one. Then in the five or six days preceding the special day start mailing them, one at a time, to your honey. This tells her you're thinking ahead (always a welcome revelation to your woman), and you build her anticipation for the special day—a tried and tested method of telling a woman you really love her.

Don't buy her sexy lingerie for Valentine's Day or any other special occasion. That's mainly a gift for you and it tells her what she already suspects—you know, that old "the only thing on his mind is…." And you know buying something "practical" for her—like a blender or a can opener or a new set of snow tires–doesn't cut it either. Instead, buy her a little something that's unusual. Maybe some specially flavored tea or coffee. Maybe a different kind of perfume (but keep the receipt in case you guess wrong!). Look in an antique shop for some old time Valentines or any heart-shaped object. Put a little thought in it. Candy and flowers are fine, but they are a bit routine and thoughtful love breaks out of the routine.

On the days preceding that notable date plant little love notes around the house or hide them in her purse. Tuck them in places where she'll find them unexpectedly. You might sneak some into her car—tape them to the rear view mirror or the speedometer. Write a love note on a post-it note and put it in her check register or on one of her credit cards. She'll find them when she's checking out at a store, and she'll be delightedly embarrassed at your spontaneity and sneakiness.

Make some advance plans for your celebration—and let your sweetheart know about them *ahead of time.* Once again, anticipation is a key part of romance. Don't take it for granted that she's going to be your Valentine or that she'll be free the evening of the 14th. Call her early in the week. Ask her if she'll be your Valentine. Ask her if she's busy Saturday night. Then tell her something about your suggested plans for the evening. *Warning: this does require advance thought. Don't call her up and say "what do you want to do?" That tells her you don't have anything planned—which means you didn't care enough to plan—which means you're not thinking about her—which means—well, you get the picture. So plan ahead.* Have something in mind when you call her. But be flexible and don't get your feelings hurt if she has an alternative idea to share. Flex your plan, not just your muscles.

Give her some coupons for tasks or activities you don't normally like to do. Maybe a coupon to spend a few hours shopping with her (I know, this is a really sacrificial gift). Give her a coupon to wash her car and fill it with gas, or to do some dreaded household chores, or to read her poetry by the fireplace. Just remember to follow through and really do those things when she calls the coupon in.

So there they are, guys. Helpful hints to avoid the "anniversary effect" and hit the bull's eye on Valentine's Day. Hopefully your arrow will find its mark and you'll effectively communicate your love to the woman in your life. Good luck and have a happy Valentine's Day!

31

Guard Your Heart

They were two people apparently in love. They enjoyed each other's company and, for her, it was a welcome retreat to be in his arms after a long stressful day at work. For him, she was exciting, interesting and challenging. It might have been a wonderful relationship at another time or in another place. But for Air Force Lieutenant Kelli Flinn it was the very worst time and in the very worst place. America's first female bomber pilot—one who had performed so admirably at the academy and in her service—found herself facing court martial for violating the Air Force's stringent rules against adultery, lying and refusing to obey an order to stop seeing her married lover.

Much has been written and said about Kelli Flinn and the Air Force's handling of her situation. Whatever your opinion about the merits of her case, one thing can be agreed upon: Adultery hurts. In ancient Israel the marriage vow of fidelity was deemed extremely sacred, and adultery was punishable by death. The sacredness of the marriage vow is no less important today than it was centuries ago. How many marriages have been dissolved because one partner or the other gave in to a moment of temptation and let a rush of hormones and emotions override reason and integrity? How many children are growing up in single parent homes because the vow of fidelity was carelessly cast aside? There is hope, however, for those who want to keep their marriages intact and build a hedge against adultery. The truth is that we can and must daily discipline ourselves against the temptation to commit adultery by guarding our hearts in the following ways:

Recognize reality. There are places you shouldn't go, movies and magazines you shouldn't see and people you shouldn't hang around. Don't permit yourself to linger in compromising situations. If you do, you'll be setting yourself up for a fall. Recognize the reality of temptations and do your best to avoid them.

Discipline your thought life. Martin Luther, the Reformation theologian (and one time law student!) said, "You can't keep birds from flying over your head but you can keep them from building a nest in your hair." The same goes for your thought life. If your thoughts begin to carry you down the wrong road, do a U-turn. Force your focus on something else. Be mentally tough on yourself. A little discipline now will reap benefits for years to come.

Don't stand on the fence. When you go to Niagara Falls you will hardly ever see anyone standing on top of the fence that separates the Falls from the safe walkways surrounding it. That's because it's dangerous to be on the fence. You could slip into the Falls and lose your life. Ditto for your lifestyle. Don't flirt (literally) with disaster by what you say or do with members of the opposite sex. The path to adultery is usually a gentle slope underfoot. Most people end up in an adulterous relationship by taking small steps—an intimate conversation with your married co-worker, followed by a lingering lunch, and a seemingly innocent drink after work. You can avoid the downhill slope by staying off the fence. Watch your words, your winks and your wayward glances.

Assert control over your emotions. Your *will* can control your *emotions.* Once you take the vow of marital fidelity you must decide to close your heart to that attractive person of the opposite sex. Resolve not to be alone with that individual if you fear the temptation is more than you can handle. When emotions well up and threaten to take over, assert control over your feelings by making right decisions. It's not always the "fun" thing to do, but it's always the right thing to do. Make the choice of fidelity and integrity, not the choice of false intimacy.

Start from today. If you've given in to temptation in the past and broken your vow of fidelity, don't despair and give up. If you've blown it in the past, you can start anew today with a fresh vow of fidelity. Adopt the Marine Corp's motto as your personal pledge: *Semper fi*—always faithful. Make it part of your life from this point forward and commit to being a person of fidelity from this day onward.

Finally, a word to those suffering from the effects of unfaithfulness in their marriage: the hurt can be healed but it will take time. If your spouse is willing to reconcile, try to find it in your heart to forgive. Get counseling and allow the healing process to begin. And take care not to let their unfaithfulness be an excuse for your own. With time and forgiveness your marriage can be restored.

Lt. Kelly Flinn was an example for young females all across America. She showed how a woman can serve well in the armed forces. Now she serves as an example for all of us. Don't let unfaithfulness cause you to bomb out. Be a person of high fidelity. Stay faithful and guard your heart.✠

32

Give Away Apples of Gold for Valentine's Day

Jo Ann and Larry were just an ordinary couple. Nothing special about them really. They struggled to make the house payment, just like you and me. They worked hard and went to bed tired at the end of the day, just like you and me. And they had their share of marital squabbles, just like you and me. Just an ordinary couple—until one day Larry did something extraordinary. He started complimenting Jo Ann.

At first, it was the "magic drawer" Larry said he discovered. "Thanks, Jo Ann, for my magic drawer. Seems every time I go there, it's magically filled with clean socks that you've placed in there after doing the laundry. Thanks."

At first Jo Ann was suspicious. Wouldn't you be? "What do you want, Larry?" was her initial response. "Nothing," said Larry. "I just wanted to thank you for my clean socks." But Jo Ann was still suspicious.

After that the compliments seemed to come in a variety of shapes and forms. Thanks for keeping the check book balanced. Thanks for the 14,000 meals you've cooked over the years. Thanks for the work you do around the house.

It got so "bad" Jo Ann's daughter said her dad was even complimenting *her*. "Dad's gone bonkers, Mom. He's not himself anymore. He just told me I looked nice." "Hmmm, strange behavior," thought Jo Ann.

But Jo Ann's initial skepticism and raised eyebrows began to give way to a responsive smile and even a few "Thanks for the compliment, Larry." After awhile Jo Ann said her step became a little lighter, her self-confidence seemed higher, and once in a while she even caught herself humming. She didn't seem to be as blue anymore either. But what really startled Jo Ann was when she heard these words coming out of her mouth, "Larry, thanks for going to work and providing for us all these years. I don't think I've ever told you how much I appreciate it."

Larry never did tell Jo Ann why he started behaving so strangely—even though she bugged him to tell her. She's finally just chalked it up to one of life's mysteries and decided to enjoy and participate in it. Wouldn't we all like to enjoy that kind of mystery?

We can. There are countless little things we encounter every day within our families that we can compliment or thank someone for. Valentine's Day is a great time to start this verbal love-in. If your brain is stuck on where to begin, start with some of Larry's ideas–simple things like socks, and meals and checkbooks. Make sure your compliments are sincere—not just puffing and fluff. Most folks can detect a real compliment from an insincere one, so make yours the real thing.

You'll probably encounter some early opposition. Your compliment recipient may be like Jo Ann and say, "What's the catch?" Don't let that deter you from your mission. And what is your mission on this crusade of complimenting? Simply this: to lighten someone's step, to increase someone's self-esteem, to give someone a reason to hum, to paint their world in a color other than blue.

You may or may not get a compliment in return. You may just get a lot of raised eyebrows. But you'll be living out the truth recorded thousands of years ago by Solomon, the wisest man of all time. "Like apples of gold in settings of silver is a word spoken in right circumstances." Why not give your loved one a gold apple for Valentine's Day—and every day thereafter?

33

Divorce is Too Easy
an Option

She was a delightful young lady in her mid 20s with a
gentle smile and a friendly face. As I sat beside her in the
plane coming back from Atlanta, we struck up a conversation that ranged through a variety of topics. Predictably,
our talk wound its way to our homes and our families. "I'm
divorced," she said matter-of-factly. "Actually not divorced—
we're separated, but we still see each other and we're still
good friends."

"I don't mean to stick my nose in where it doesn't belong,"
I said to her, "but have you and your husband tried counseling?" "Well, we went to a pastor," she replied, "and he
told us we were approaching this very maturely." I winced
inside. Why wasn't this pastor fighting to save this marriage? Why such a cavalier attitude about divorce? I pressed
ahead. "There's an excellent marriage seminar coming to
Oklahoma City the second week-end in November spon-
sored by Family Life Ministries—would you and your husband consider going?" I asked. "We might," she said
thoughtfully. "Send me some information about it."

Marriage is more than a relationship of convenience. It's
more than a contract. It's even more than a promise made
before witnesses. Marriage is a sacred institution. God put
it bluntly in Malachi 2:16, "I hate divorce," and Jesus reit-
erated the same thought in Matthew 19:6, "What God has
joined together let no man put asunder." The Bible is

pretty clear about this concept: God is in favor of lifetime marital commitments, and He hates their dissolution.

How can it happen, then, that over 50% of marriages in the United States end in divorce? Why does Oklahoma City and Oklahoma County top the list in per capita divorces? Why has America—and Oklahoma in particular–strayed so far from the original design of marriage, a lifetime commitment? Here are a few of the reasons:

No fault divorce laws now make it too easy to dissolve the bonds of matrimony. In order to obtain a divorce no "fault" need be alleged and there is no requirement that the other marriage partner agree. Most of the divorces in Oklahoma are granted on grounds of "incompatibility." As a society we let people out of their marriage promises easier than we let them out of a contract to join a health club. Divorce is too easy to obtain under current laws.

Divorce is treated lightly. Hallmark® stores sell cards that congratulate the newly divorced individual on regaining their freedom. Television and movies yawn at divorce and treat it as simply a way of life. Even in the church there is little that communicates the tragedy of divorce. Sadly, the divorce rate for people attending church is not much different from those who do not attend. And even though three quarters of American marriages occur in churches, the church has done little to stem the rising tide of divorce. Instead of taking a united stand and setting minimum standards before engaged couples can be married, many of our houses of worship have become little more than "blessing factories"— just another pretty place to hold a wedding.

Little is being done to address the root causes of divorce. Who are the likely candidates for divorce? Those who marry too young, those who get pregnant too early, those without communication and conflict resolution skills, those without role models, those with financial struggles and those without someone to whom they can turn in a marital crisis. There is much that can and should be done to address these problems, and the place to begin is in the churches.

The empirical evidence is in. Divorce is not good for husbands, for wives, for children or for our society. It contributes to poverty and low self-esteem in children and results in poorer health and a recurring sense of failure in adults. Society pays the cost associated with divorced parents who fail or refuse to pay child support, increased costs of welfare and lower productivity among the divorce casualties. Divorce costs a lot—and the amount you pay the lawyer and in the settlement is only the beginning.

34

Celebrating Valentine's Day

When I was growing up (some say I still haven't!) I remember my mom celebrating nearly every holiday, no matter its significance. We used to have a calendar in our kitchen that had little pictures on important dates in history. For example on June 3rd (my birthday) there was a little picture of Jefferson Davis, the president of the Confederacy, because that was his birthday too. In our house any day that had a little picture on the calendar merited a celebration. We always decorated the house or gave gifts or baked something special in honor of the day.

February was one of my favorite months to celebrate because we decorated for three special days: Washington's birthday, Lincoln's birthday and Valentine's Day. Back in those days school let out for both Washington's birthday *and* Lincoln's birthday so every kid had a reason to celebrate! Mom would bake cherry squares in honor of Washington's chopped-down cherry tree, and pictures of George and Abraham adorned our home. We also celebrated Valentine's Day. For us it wasn't just a time for romantic couples—it was also a celebration of family love. We bought or made Valentine cards for each other, gave gifts of flowers or candy (conversation hearts were always my favorite) and saw lots of pictures of red hearts and cupids around the house. I don't remember my mom and dad going out on a date on Valentine's Day, but I know they did some kind of mushy, romantic things like hugging and kissing. Even though all that kissing seemed kind of gross to a young boy of ten,

I always felt good about the way they showed affection toward each other.

Maybe that's why I'm an advocate of celebrating, especially in the month of February. I still haul out the pictures of Abraham Lincoln and George Washington and tack them up somewhere in our house. We also make a big deal about Valentine's Day. Lots of cards and red hearts and flowers and candy—lots of candy—will adorn our house this year. And I'm also a strong advocate of showing affection by both words and deeds.

If I could pass some legislation about Valentine's Day celebrations in our homes, my list of "must-do's" would look like this:

> You must tape up several large red hearts around your home to remind everyone to show love to each other.

> You must buy a generous supply of candy, conversation hearts and leave them in unexpected places for others in your family to find and read the messages.

> You must write secret love notes to those you love and hide them where they'll find them later. Tucked in a wallet or purse, hung by the car keys on a hook, taped on the bathroom mirror, or hidden in a shoe.

> You must make, not buy, a Valentine's card for your sweetheart. Even if you're not a great poet, a homemade poem is still the best gift you can give.

You must properly prepare for the big day. Remind each other that Valentine's Day is coming. Build the anticipation. Send cards in the mail for a few days ahead of time.

You must buy or make something to give to each member of your family on February 14. Even dads should give gifts to their sons and moms to their daughters. Nothing expensive. Just a little something that expresses the love in your heart.

Obviously Valentine's Day shouldn't be the only time you express love to your family members, but it can be a special time you celebrate the love and take the time to say it and show it in a tangible way. I know sometimes it's not easy to say "I love you," and those words come more easily to some folks than others. Still, Valentine's Day provides the perfect opportunity, and the perfect excuse, to communicate our love for those in the family. Don't be like those greeting cards in the Hallmark® store that read, "I know I don't tell you very often how much you mean to me...." Instead, celebrate the love in your family.

And if your family isn't feeling all that loving right now, use Valentine's Day as an opportunity to rekindle the spark of affection. Our actions will always lead our emotions, so we must begin acting in a loving way even if the feelings aren't there at first. I can almost guarantee that if you begin acting toward a person in a loving manner, you will feel more affectionate toward that person. It's not easy, but it's worth the effort.

So go ahead. Hang up a few red hearts. Buy those conversation hearts. Hide those love notes in a shoe. Celebrate family love this Valentine's Day!

✛ ✛ ✛

35

A Steadfast Commitment

Alzheimer's had stolen the twinkle in her eye and her warm, engaging smile. She was sinking deeper and deeper into the grasp of a living kind of death where she neither knew those around her nor could respond to their gestures of love and concern. Caring for her had become increasingly burdensome for her husband who was trying to juggle a demanding job as president of a major institution while giving his beloved wife time and love and tenderness.

At last he had to make a choice. His responsibilities at work tore him one way, and his concern for his wife pulled him the other. He rose one day to address the Board of Trustees at their monthly meeting and informed them of his decision to resign. He was needed full time at home and he could not do justice to the institution as its president when his heart was far away. His place was at his wife's side in these last months.

A well-meaning trustee approached him during a break in the meeting to talk him out of his decision. The trustee's intentions were good, but his insight was lacking. "There are two things I want to tell you about this situation," the trustee said. "First, there are others who can care for your wife besides you and second, she doesn't even know who you are anyway." "I know," said the president, "but *I* know who *she* is." And with that he confirmed his decision to step down.

Robertson McQuilkin resigned his position to care for his wife Muriel in her final days. Do we have that same level of commitment to those whom we love? Do we have the kind of relationship that bears up in the storms of life and tempest-tossed emotions, or do we possess a fair weather love, dependent on good feelings, good times and good finances? The ancient Hebrew language has a word for love called *hisson*. It literally means "steadfast commitment." It's sometimes translated "loyalty" as in the Old Testament book of Proverbs, chapter 21, verse 21, "He who pursues righteousness and loyalty (love) finds life and righteousness and honor." For the Hebrews, love was not a feeling that waxed and waned with the mood of the moment. It represented a loyal commitment, a steadfast promise, a covenant "for better or for worse." Hmmm, seems like I've heard that phrase somewhere before.

Oh, I remember. It was in my own wedding vows, and if you were married in a typical ceremony it was probably in yours. That kind of steadfast commitment stands in stark contrast to the on again, off again commitments of convenience that too often punctuate our relationships in today's world. For too many of us love is more often defined by the highly memorable beer commercial where a manipulative guy tells everyone and anyone, "I love ya man" just to get a can of beer. Funny commercial. Sad commentary on our society. Maybe it hits too close to home with some of us. Have we professed "love" for others but been unwilling to make the sacrifices of time and self that inevitably go along with it?

Love is not a feeling. It's a decision we make everyday. Sometimes the feelings associated with love are good, the music is right, we have a little money in our pocket and the sun is shining outside. All's right with the world. But sometimes the feelings of love are faint, the music is off key, our last quarter just slipped through the hole in our pocket and the sky is leaden gray. At those times in our relationships, love hasn't died. It's just calling for a decision. It's calling for a little deeper commitment. It's calling for us to dig into our Hebrew-English dictionary and pull out the Hebrew word *hisson*—"steadfast commitment." It's calling us to be like Marines in our relationships: *Semper fi*—always faithful.

I don't always feel like doing this, and if you're human (and honest) you probably don't either. There are days I don't especially feel like being loving. I'd rather kick the cat, take a long drive and shirk whatever responsibility or duty is irritatingly calling to me. You probably have days like that too. It's on those days we have to act better than we feel. We have to decide to choose commitment over feelings. Feelings are fickle. They rise and fall on a whim. Our lives and our relationships have to be based on something stronger than that. Relationships need to be based on steadfast commitment. They need to be rooted in love. They need to be founded on the kind of thing that makes a man like Robertson McQuilkin resign his post because he knows who his wife is, and he knows she needs him. We need more *hisson* in our relationships—with our spouse, our children, our parents and with others whom we love.

But how do we do it? We begin by reaffirming our steadfast commitment to those we love. Say it out loud; "I love you," or "Whatever happens I'll be here for you." Promise your children, "No matter what happens, your mom and I are never going to get a divorce." Tough words to say. Tough words to mean. But we begin keeping promises when we make them out loud.

The next part is both simple and hard. In the words of the Nike® commercial, "Just do it." If you've made a promise, just keep it. If your moral conscience tells you to do something, just listen. If you've taken a vow, just honor it. There's nothing glamorous or exciting about consistency, but it does pay long-term dividends. Just ask Cal Ripken. Just ask Robertson McQuilkin.

Finally, if you've blown it in the past, don't give up on yourself. Don't succumb to the temptation of discouragement and defeat that says, *"Aw, just give it up, you've broken those promises and commitments before, you'll never be able to keep them."* You can make a fresh commitment and start over. As the Old Testament book of Proverbs 24:16 says, "The righteous man falls down seven times, and yet gets up." It doesn't say a righteous man never falls—it just says he keeps getting up when he does fall. If you've fallen down on your commitments to those you love, don't despair. Just get up and renew your resolve to keep your promises one day at a time.

Wouldn't it be great if the love we share with our family and friends became a steadfast commitment? God help us find that kind of love, and God help us give that kind of love to others.

36

Acting Better than You Feel

After years of marital difficulty Ben and Michelle decided to seek counseling. And at their counselor's suggestion they brought their young daughter Meredith to one session. The subject turned to what bothered the little girl most about her home. "When Daddy and Mommy are arguing, and Daddy takes off his wedding ring and throws it across the room," said Meredith. Ben flustered an explanation, "I don't really mean anything by that—it's just a way of expressing my feelings." But Ben's way of "expressing his feelings" was sending a clear if unintended message to his daughter. His marriage commitment was something he could throw away.

Feelings are the uncontested champion of people's lives today. Most of us do things—or don't do things—because of feelings. How many times have you heard or said the expression, "But I don't feel like it." How many commercials have you seen or heard that focus on this slippery little emotional eel. Mazda® says, "It just feels right." Toyota® chimes in—"Oh what a feeling!" Beer distributors parade a lot of young, good looking, flat-bellied, tanned and lovely beach goers to convince us if we buy their brand of beer we'll feel a lot better.

Feelings sometimes rule family relations too. "I don't feel like being married anymore," says a husband. "I don't feel like handling the responsibility for these kids," says a mom. "I don't feel like obeying you!" yells the child. Feelings overtake us at every turn.

Don't get me wrong. I'm not against good feelings. I've felt good and I've felt bad, and it's most definitely better to feel good. But if we base our code of conduct on our feelings, we're building our life on sinking sand. Feelings are not to be trusted. Feelings are fickle. They change with the weather, our mood, even what we eat. They can grow hot or turn cold and sometimes disappear altogether. We cannot let our lives be run by our feelings, and we can't refuse to do things because we don't *feel* like it. *We have to act better than we feel.*

This is not popular stuff. In the hopes of popularizing this concept I had the idea of putting it on a bumper sticker so the phrase might catch on. You know, some flashy little color scheme with the phrase, "Ya Gotta Act Better Than Ya Feel" emblazoned across it. I figured it had to sell at least as well as "If you can read this bumper sticker you're too darn close," or "If you don't like my driving get off the sidewalk." But I suspect my bumper sticker idea wouldn't stick because it flies in the face of popular sentiment. Putting responsibility and duty ahead of personal satisfaction doesn't have much appeal.

But "acting better than you feel" does have a lot to do with sticking together as a family. Placing duty and responsibility above feelings is the kind of seed that produces the fruit of trust and commitment in a marriage where husband and wife are faithful to their vows and neither adultery nor divorce are options. It gives birth to the notion that kids can count on their dad or mom to follow through on promises, and their parents won't walk out on the family when thegoing gets tough. It's the kind of cement that holds together a fragile family relationship when it would be easier to break up, bail out, or go bankrupt. Acting better than you feel—what a concept to practice in our own lives and to teach our families.

The next time you don't "feel" like doing something you know you should do, just give yourself a little push and do it anyway. Will it be easy? No, it won't. But will it be the right thing to do? You bet. You'll be living and teaching your family an important life lesson about commitment and duty in a feeling-based society. And who knows? You might just feel better once you've done it.

37

We Need to Persevere in Mid-Life Marriages

If you've read this column very often you know I'm high on marriage and down on divorce. In the last thirty years we have, as a society, taken a "marriage-light" approach to our matrimonial vows. Couples seem to be a third less committed to making their marriages work. This is true for newly married couples as well as those who tied the knot long ago. Although statistics indicate a couple is most likely to divorce in the first few years of marriage, still, the number of divorces occurring among mid-life marriages is troubling. Why would someone get divorced after twenty or so years of marriage? One reason is that mid-life crisis thing. Many times (although not always) it's the husband who abandons his wife for a younger woman because he can't or won't deal with the changes in his mid-life wife. Consider this letter I received not long ago.

Dear Mr. Priest,

You asked for questions that I'd like to see answered. Here is what I would like to see: an article on menopause and how men can work through this with their wife. Some women just breeze through this time of their life, and then there are those like me who are really having a rough time with depression, sleeplessness, no sex drive, etc. Yes, I've been to the doctor. It doesn't help when your husband of 25 years says he has been really miserably unhappy for two years and wants a divorce. Do you men think that we can wave a magic wand and be 18 again? Why can't you understand that this change is unavoidable? Why don't you try to understand that I can't help it? I've been to the doctor and I'm doing the best I can. This is not a permanent condition. It will be over someday, and I will be a new person again. I guess you think a new honey is the cure for you.

Jim, it's too late for me but an article along this line might just be what someone else needs to hear, and he might go home with a totally new attitude toward his wife, thus saving a marriage. See, my husband has filed for divorce and in a month I'll be single and 50 years old and "free." My husband will have his freedom and his honey. Would you pray for me? I do not want to harbor bitterness. Pray that I give my husband to the Lord and forgive and that this menopause will get easier.

Please do not use my name.

I keep this letter to remind me to pray for this woman and to remind me about the awful trauma of divorce. I must admit, I don't know anything about what this woman is going through. But I do know she and her husband have invested 25 years in a marriage and that investment now appears to be gone. What can husbands and wives do to persevere through the sometimes difficult middle years of marriage?

– Recognize that you're going through a time of readjustment. Physical changes are taking place. Menopause is hitting women. The "bald, fat and slow" disease is hitting most men. These physical changes will also change the way you think and feel. Be ready for it and remember that these changes can be successfully handled. Many, many couples have done and are still doing it today.

– Many times mid-life marriages are also adjusting to the empty nest. Formerly, the kids took most of your energy and attention. Now you're "forced" into spending more time with each other. This adjustment is not unlike the adjustment you made when you first got married. Get to know each other. Attend a Marriage Encounter weekend (even if you don't feel like it—do it anyway!). Invest the same time and energy to re-acquaint yourself with your spouse as you would a new friend. Don't assume you still know who you're married to.

– Stick with it. There come a number of times in every marriage where you weigh the pros and cons and wonder if the cons don't outweigh the pros. It's then you need to dig in and work a bit harder. A divorce and a new spouse will probably not solve the problems with which you're struggling. The divorce statistics on second marriages are worse than for first marriages. Don't trade your old problems for new ones—work hard to resolve the old ones.

– Finally, be patient and understanding with your spouse. In our instant, microwave age we expect all problems to be solved in the span of a 30-minute television show (less commercials). Life isn't that neat and tidy. Most problems tend to work out more slowly and less predictably than they do on television. But the satisfaction of celebrating that 50th wedding anniversary and the example you provide for future generations makes the struggle worthwhile.

Mid-life marriage isn't always easy. It requires attention and work and stick-to-itiveness. But with effort and prayer your mid-life marriage can be a source of joy and fulfillment for you, *and* an encouragement and inspiration to others. Press on! Future generations will thank you for your faithfulness to the marital vows.

Parenting

family talk

38

Effective Parents Commit Themselves to Their Children

In his outstanding book, *The Seven Secrets of Effective Fathers,* author Ken Canfield tells the story of Oliver DeVinck. Oliver was stricken with a severe disability when he was only a few months old. He became blind. He could not hold up his head or crawl. He could not talk or hold anything in his hands. He was severely brain damaged. The doctor suggested that Oliver's parents place him in an institution, but Jose and Catherine DeVinck refused. "He is our son. We will take him home," said Jose. "Then take him home and love him," the doctor replied. And they did. For thirty-three years.

After Oliver passed away, Jose's other son Christopher asked his father, "How did you manage to care for Oliver for thirty-three years?" His dad replied, "It was not thirty-three years. I just asked myself, 'Can I feed Oliver today?' and the answer always was 'Yes, I can.' "

Other dedicated and loving parents might have made another decision, but the DeVincks believed Oliver's place was in their home. Few of us will be called upon to make the same commitment as Jose and Catherine DeVinck, but our commitment to our children must be no less devoted and intense. Effective parents are those who claim their children as their own and maintain long-term commitments to them. To be truly effective parents we can learn a few lessons from the DeVincks.

Jose said "He is our son." To be truly effective parents we need to make the same kind of statement. We must claim our children as our own, and one of the simple ways we can do this is by the way we introduce them to friends and strangers. When we are talking to our friends and our child walks up beside us, do we forget they are there and make no introductions? Do we offhandedly say, "This is my son Chad," and then hurry back to "adult" conversation? If so, we fail to claim our children in a way that communicates to them—and to others—we're proud to be their parents. Be sure to proudly introduce your child and comment on some interesting thing about them or their activities. They may blush or look embarrassed momentarily, but they will catch the message you're communicating: "You are connected with me!"

I remember my grandmother constantly referred to members of her family as "*our* Jim" or "*our* Tom." That's the way she would introduce us to others. There was something special about that little word "our" that connected me to Gram. It was the feeling that if I ever needed anything she'd be there for me. I knew she loved me even without her saying so, but her words cemented the fact immovably in my mind. She constantly reminded us what an important part of her family we were until we really began to believe it. We can do the same thing with our children by verbally affirming their importance in our lives and telling them how proud we are to be their parents.

Jose DeVinck said, "We will take Oliver home." This simple sentence signified the commitment to be there for Oliver and to integrate his life with the family's life. While we may never be faced with a severely handicapped child we can still make the commitment to integrate our life with our child's life. Staying aware of our children's daily joys and disappointments is one way. Do you know the names of your child's best friends? Do you know who their best (and worst) teachers are at school? Do you know their greatest fear—or their proudest moment—or their favorite song? These are questions that are not answered in a hurried goodbye moment or while grabbing a quick kiss good night at bed time. To be integrated in our children's life requires us to slow down and talk with them in unrushed moments. This applies even after they are grown. We have to make a conscious effort to "take our children home."

Finally, Jose said he made the commitment to his son one day at a time. We need to do the same. The word "commit" actually means to "hand over" or "entrust," and that's what we must do every day. We are called to "hand over" at least part of our time and energy for the building of our children. Even though we know this truism, we Americans fail to commit much time to our children. Surprisingly, statistics indicate that children in the United States spend less time with their parents than children in any other country in the world. In the former Soviet Union, for example, fathers spend an average of more than two hours a day with their children, compared with less than *thirty-seven seconds* a day for dads in the United States. No matter how many times you've read *The One Minute Manager*, it's hard to have an impact in thirty-seven seconds a day! We simply must make the commitment to take the time to be involved on a day-by-day basis. It's not easy, but it is a time investment that reaps handsome dividends in family relations.

You can begin today with a DeVinck-like commitment

to spend the time and energy necessary to truly parent your child, whatever the cost. Claim them as your own. Integrate your life with theirs. Commit the time and energy necessary. Jose would tell you, it's time well spent.

39

Honoring Your Children is Important

"Go sit on the bench and don't move from there until I tell you!" the coach yelled at the young football player. "I'm sick and tired of your bad attitude, and if you think I'm going to put up with that you're crazy!"

The young man, humiliated and dejected, dragged himself to the bench and sat down in a slump. It was bad enough to be yelled at by the coach, but it was even worse when the coach was your dad. For the next hour the young man sat on the bench while his father/coach forgot about him and worked with the rest of the team. Only after practice was over did his dad remember the exiled son and release him from his pine prison. "And don't ever embarrass me like that again," his dad said as he walked away from the boy whose head was still hanging and whose face was streaked with tears.

Maybe the kid did have a bad attitude. But the dad forgot an important lesson that works in both fathering and coaching, "Don't dishonor your children."

Much has been said—and rightly so—about the important concept of honoring your mother and father. The Biblical commandment is an important truth that all people, young and old, ought to observe. But the Bible also talks about showing honor to *all* people, even the children whom we are called to discipline, nurture and correct.

There are many ways parents can dishonor their children. Making fun of the things your child takes seriously. Poking fun at their friends. Not listening to their opinions. Embarrassing them in public by the way we talk to them or discipline them, like the father/coach in our story.

I don't always act wisely with my own children. Sometimes I mess up and over-react. Sometimes I speak out of anger. Sometimes I forget to "praise in public and criticize in private." It's on those days I need to remember the command of the Apostle Paul in the New Testament book of Ephesians: "Fathers, do not exasperate your children, but bring them up in the discipline and instruction of the Lord." I need to do less exasperating and more of the disciplining and instructing in the Lord. You probably do too.

So parents should show honor to their children and treat their feelings with respect. We can do this by:

– Listening—really listening—when our children are talking about something important to them. Ask them questions and listen with both your ears and your eyes. Put your newspaper down or turn the TV off for a few minutes and really listen.

– Don't speak about your children in a demeaning or discouraging way in public. Saying things like, "You know Johnny's not very good in math," or "I just can't seem to teach him good manners" sends our children the wrong message. Instead, praise them in public.

– Discipline and correct your children, yes—but whenever possible do it in a way that avoids embarrassing them. Sometimes we need to take immediate and strong action with our kids, but many times we can correct them out of the public eye. If possible take them to the side or out of the room to administer a verbal reprimand or spanking. Criticize in private.

– Make sure your children know you're proud of them. You can purchase a special "red dinner plate" at most department stores which says, "This is your special day." Put the red plate out on birthdays, special occasions or just to let your kids know you're glad to be their parent. Put their pictures or artwork up at the office, on the refrigerator, or display them proudly in the living room.

– Every once in a while tell your kids: "What did I do right to deserve such a great kid as you?" They'll blush and think it's corny, but inside they'll feel ten feet tall.

I try to use this rule of thumb when I'm dealing with my kids: Is this the way I want them to treat me when they come visit me in the nursing home thirty or forty years from now? Do I want them to just order me around, yell at me for my senile behavior and embarrass me in front of my senior friends? Or do I want them to treat me with honor and respect and dignity?

Don't send your kid to the bench in embarrassment. Discipline them when they need it, but always, always honor them by treating them with respect.

139

40

Honoring Your Parents is Important

Joanne had a turbulent and abusive childhood. Her alcoholic father would angrily lash out at her verbally and physically when he was in a drunken tirade. Her mother never seemed strong enough to intervene. Joanne moved out as soon as she was old enough, and after her parents divorced while she was in college, she had no interest in ever seeing her dad again.

She dove into her career and thought she had shut the door on her unhappy past. But after reading her Bible and talking with a close friend, Joanne realized she was carrying a heavy load of bitterness and anger toward her father. She had difficulty controlling her temper and found it hard to trust God and those around her. Joanne finally decided she had to find her father and try to reconcile with him.

Through family and friends Joanne located her dad living alone in an apartment complex in a distant city. She gathered her courage, boarded an airplane and, when she landed, made the most difficult phone call of her life. "Daddy?" she tentatively said. "Joanne, is that you?" said a tired, old voice at the other end. "Daddy, I'm in town. I came to talk to you." He hurriedly gave her directions and after an awkward second or two at the front door of his apartment, he invited her in.

They talked about small things for awhile until Joanne

finally broached the real purpose of her visit. "Daddy, I came to apologize to you. For years, I have had anger and bitterness in my heart toward you, and I came to ask your forgiveness."

"Me forgive you?" the old man asked incredulously. "I'm the one who needs to be forgiven." And as he poured out his heart full of remorse and guilt, the two shared a reconciliation Joanne had thought impossible. Through tears he offered a long overdue apology, and somehow she found it in her heart to forgive him. As years went by their relationship remained strong, although obviously far from ideal. But Joanne and her dad gained a new perspective on forgiveness and love and were able to salvage a lost family link.

Joanne took seriously the Biblical command to "honor your father and mother." This is the first commandment with a promise: "so that it may go well with you and that you may enjoy long life on the earth." At the core of all strong family relationships is "honor"—a showing of respect. The Bible talks about children honoring their parents—but also tells parents to show honor toward children. Clearly, Joanne's father did not show her honor during her childhood, and some would contend that his actions disqualified him from receiving any respect from her. But the command is unqualified. We are to show parents honor regardless of circumstance. Joanne took the first step to reconciling with her dad by "honoring" him, whether he truly deserved it or not. We should do the same.

Perhaps your childhood was like Joanne's–abusive, neglected, filled with angry words. Maybe yours was ideal–warmth, encouragement, discipline with love. Or you could have had something in between. Parents who loved you but never quite showed it or told you, or parents who never quite found enough time to spend with you. Whatever your background, *you* hold the key to a potential reconciliation by honoring your parents.

It may not be easy. You may meet with initial resistance from your folks. You may think it impossible to re-build a bridge that was long ago burned. But as you take the initial steps to honor your parents you'll find the road less difficult than you thought. God will reward your efforts to be faithful to the commandment, and even if the relationship is never quite repaired, you will benefit from your decision to show honor to your mother and father. Here are a few suggestions:

Don't be afraid to take the first step. Joanne could have stayed at home and complained, "Let HIM apologize to ME, he's the one who did wrong." She'd have been right, but she probably would still be waiting for him to call. As a practical matter it's of no consequence who makes the initial move. We may have to swallow our pride a little by taking the first step, but that lump in your throat won't compare to the one you get embracing a lost parent.

Learn about your parents' background. If we learn something about our parents' upbringing it often helps us understand why they acted as they did. Do a little digging. Talk with them or other family members about your parents' growing up years. It may give you some insight that will help build your relationship with them.

Open the lines of communication. Perhaps it has been years since you've talked with your parents. You might consider writing a letter, making a phone call, or better yet, an in person visit. But begin to establish the communication connection and strive to keep the line open.

Don't expect instant reconciliation. While Joanne's story is true, many broken relationships take a longer time to heal. Be patient and don't give up. Even if your parents refuse to respond, gently persist in love. Chances are that if you make a sincere and continuous effort they will ultimately open up to you.

God's commandment is clear, and He will make you adequate to carry out this important directive. Take the first step toward honoring your father and your mother. They'll be glad you did and so will you.

___

Parental Anger

I'm going to make a statement I hope will not be misunderstood: *I never really understood child abuse until I had children.* Now having said that let me hasten to add I strongly oppose child abuse. But the fact remains that there were times, when our kids were young and crying incessantly, that I began to understand how little kids can make sane men and women crazy with frustration and anger.

I was sitting on the sofa one day, holding my darling little Amanda when, without warning, she hauled off and punched me very hard in the nose. I don't know about your nose, but my nose is very sensitive and a well-placed fist brings a sensation to it that is akin to being poked in the eye with a stick. After being brutally assaulted like that my first instinct was to rear back and pop her one on her own nose. Fortunately I stopped. I realized, this is the little girl I love most in the world. How could I even think about hitting her? Still, her childish behavior almost brought out the worst in me.

Kids will do things that rile you. Little kids, especially, seem to enjoy testing the limits of authority and, having found the limits, promptly exceed them. They will be self-centered. They will pout and stomp their feet. They will pitch a fit in the grocery store in an effort to thoroughly embarrass you into giving them whatever their selfish little minds have fixated on.

Your natural reaction will be to strike back. To yell when they yell. To hit when they hit. To be as selfish to them as they are to you. But, as an adult, you have to remember three words of sage advice: "Don't do it!"

Restraining anger is one of the hallmarks of a mature person. Believe me, there's nothing that requires more maturity than life as a parent. A parent must fight the natural instinct to look out for one's self and, instead, act selflessly.

Here's some helpful tips for parents who feel themselves tipping over the edge of anger with their kids:

Give yourself a break. When babies or toddlers are crying, remember to keep things in perspective. If their diaper is dry, they've been fed and they don't appear hurt, it's ok to just let them cry for awhile. Even if you have to leave them (safely) in their room or crib for a short while (while you compose yourself), don't feel the need to drop everything you're doing at the drop of a tear.

Restrain yourself. There will be times in the early childhood years when you'll get so frustrated you'll feel like yelling, throwing things, running out of the house and generally losing control. You will probably be tempted to spank your children out of anger more than out of a desire to properly discipline them. Find some other outlet for those feelings of frustrations, but don't take them out on the kids. Remember, you're the adult—the (supposedly) mature one. Try to act like it.

Watch your words. The Old Testament book of Proverbs says, "A gentle answer turns away wrath but a harsh word stirs up trouble." We all know this truth from our own lives. When parents begin yelling out harsh words it usually spells trouble for harmony in the home. Control your mouth, and don't lash your kids with your tongue.

Keep things in perspective. Most of our problems with little children aren't as earth shattering as they seem at the time. If your son has taken a playmate's candy bar, it doesn't mean he'll grow up to be John Dillinger. Nevertheless, while you keep things in perspective, remember you're in the process of "building" an adult. You don't want to be as inflexible as a two-by-four, but you don't want to be like a strand of cooked spaghetti either. Major on majors and lighten up on minors.

Show your children honor. Even in disciplining your children, try to show them honor and respect. This may sound hard to do when you're upending them for a spanking, but especially as kids get older, don't embarrass them in the way you punish them. Try to take your kids out of the room to impose discipline and consider their feelings when others are around watching. This isn't always possible, but when you can pay attention to this honor principle.

From time to time, most parents feel frustrated enough with their kids to totter on the brink of an anger explosion. It's then that you need to step back, cool off, maintain perspective and remember to show honor even in discipline. Keep your words and your actions gentle, and don't stir up trouble in your home.

42

Parenting is a Marathon

For the last five Augusts I have traveled south to Wichita Falls, Texas to participate in a bicycle race called the Hotter'n Hell Hundred. It's named appropriately. Temperatures usually range in the high 90s to 100s as 8,000 bikers ride through the streets and countryside surrounding this north Texas town. You can ride 25, 50, 62 or 100 miles. I usually pick the 50. It's far enough to make you feel like you accomplished something but not so far that you feel it for a week afterward.

As I was riding in the event this year I suddenly realized how much parenting is like the Hotter'n Hell. So here are some observations about biking and parenting:

Everyone bikes at their own pace. Even though all the bikers had some things in common (we all wore helmets, we all had pedals, we all were sweating), we all biked at a different pace. Some of the people who were in the bike race took off fast—and finished fast. Some guys finished the 100 mile race before I finished the 50. I finished in front of some people, behind many others. But my goal was to finish—not to beat anyone else. It's like that in parenting too. We all have some things in common, just like bikers do (we all have kids, we all have joys and frustrations, we all sweat), but we all parent at different paces. If you look around and see other parents doing things differently than you, don't panic and worry because your parenting style is different than someone else's. Find a pace and a style that fits you

147

and keep on pedaling (or parenting!).

You can see a lot by observing. This "truism" from Yogi Berra applies in both biking and parenting. I found that I saw many new things around Wichita Falls by slowing down from my usual 60-mile-an-hour car pace, to a more leisurely 15-mile-an-hour bike pace. Things that were simply a blur in a car could be seen in detail on a bike. At the rest stops, when I laid down in the grass to stretch out, I felt the warm sun, saw the blue sky overhead and vowed to slow down and lay in the grass more often this next year. It's true in parenting also. We get going too fast, most of the time, to really enjoy our kids. We're speeding along to our jobs, to the ball games, to church, to the PTA at 60 miles an hour and our life becomes a blur. When was the last time you laid in the grass with your kids and looked up at the stars at night, or the clouds during the day? "Well partner," (as the Wolf Brand® chili commercial says) "that's too long!"

It helps to train. Some years I prepare better than others for the 50-mile race. The best method is to start off doing short bike rides and gradually work your way up to long rides on the weekends. But some years I simply don't have time (this year was one of those) and when I don't train, I really feel it in my legs. The ride is harder, and the recuperation time is longer. I usually promise myself to train better next year. Ditto for parenting. I'm a better parent if I do a little training along the way. Read a book, attend a seminar, work at the little everyday things of being a good parent. If I do these things on a consistent basis, then when a "big event" comes up—a crisis to be handled or some discipline to be administered—I'm better prepared to handle it.

Sometimes, it can really be a pain you know where. This year I forgot to take my padded bicycle shorts. It was a long, hard race for my tailbone. You can probably figure out the similarity between biking and parenting on this point. Enough said.

It helps to talk along the way. This year I rode the race with my sister-in-law, Karen. As we rode we talked for hours— about our lives, our goals, books we had read lately. It was encouraging to have someone along who shared the journey and could boost my spirits when I got tired. Parenting is the same. You benefit greatly from having a "riding buddy" as you pedal through parenting. Ideally it's a husband or wife. But if your spouse is gone, you'll benefit from finding a friend or group with whom you can share your life, your goals—even the books you've read. When your spirits droop and you feel like calling the "sag wagon," your fellow travelers can give you a boost and help you push across the finish line.

Fifty miles is a marathon, not a sprint. I tried to set a measured pace so I would make it the whole 50 miles. I could have started out fast, pedaling like the wind, but I wouldn't have been able to stay the course. Parenting is a marathon too, not a sprint. You have to pedal each day, pacing yourself for the long haul, and not give in to the temptation to do something "quick and easy." It's not enough, as a parent, to begin well. You must also finish well.

When I came across the finish line this year, sweaty and tired, my children were standing there smiling and waving and cheering. It was a nice sight to see. I hope at the end of my parent race my children will also be smiling and waving and cheering. I hope I pace myself properly. I hope I slow down to observe my children's growth. I hope I will train well. I hope I've encouraged others along the race—and been encouraged by them too. At the end of my parental marathon I hope I leave behind an example of a man who faithfully stayed the course and finished the race well. As you pedal your parent bike, I hope that's your hope too. Pedal on!

43

Parents Can Teach Respect for Others by Example

One of the things that really gets under my skin is when I see people being careless with the property of other people. Graffitti written on walls, dinging a parked car and not leaving your name, shopping carts strewn all over the parking lot instead of being returned to the store. I realize we have a lot more serious problems than these, but maybe those more serious problems would be less serious if we taught our children to respect other people's property a bit more.

That's where my dad comes in. He taught me some serious lessons about taking care of the property of others. I wrote him a letter about it, thanking him for his good tutoring:

Dear Dad,

I went to the hardware store tonight, just like the million times you took me to the hardware store back home to buy some tool or do-it-yourself thing or another. I remembered how much we both enjoyed hardware stores and how we used to just nose around in them—"always something to learn" you'd tell me. I remember you saying how you'd like to own a hardware store someday, and over the years I've bought one for you a thousand times in my mind.

Anyway, I bought a bunch of stuff that I couldn't carry out to the car in one trip, so I loaded it into a shopping cart, wheeled the basket of goodies out to my car, loaded it all into the trunk and then hustled the cart back into the store, lining it up with all of its look-alike brothers and sisters. From across the store the check out lady called out, "Hey thanks a lot for bringing that back in, I appreciate it." Undoubtedly the words of one whose job it was to herd in the lost strays from the parking area after hours. "Don't thank me," I thought to myself, "Thank my dad." He's the one who taught me to put things back where I found them—or at least he tried to.

"Everything has its place and everything's in its place," you were fond of saying. And that meant not just keeping tools and books and such picked up and put away around the house—it also meant taking care to put things back that were borrowed and to return them in at least as good—if not better condition than when you borrowed them. You never borrowed things very often. I got the sense you hated to borrow things for fear they might break and you wouldn't be able to fulfill your self-imposed commitment not to wear or tear the item. I remember the time I borrowed Uncle Bill's fishing rod and reel and got the line all tangled up early one Sunday morning before church. You spent quite a bit of time untangling the line, muttering all the time, "Don't ever borrow anything again." I'm afraid I didn't keep that commandment—but I never did borrow anyone's fishing reel again—except for yours.

What you taught me was respect for other people's pro-

perty. That meant walking on the sidewalk, not cutting across the lawn. I can't remember a single time I ever saw you cut across a lawn anywhere. It also meant asking next door neighbors, Helen and George, if I could go get a baseball I had accidentally knocked over the fence into their yard instead of just jumping the fence to go get it. It meant giving other people's coats a better spot on the coat rack or washing a pan real good before you gave it back to the person who had given you a pie. Mostly it meant the golden rule—treat other's property at least as good, if not better than you would your own.

And it meant running shopping carts back into the store to their proper place rather than leaving them willy nilly in the parking lot to bang into someone's new car or to serve as an unofficial obstacle in the path of weary drivers. So the lady at the hardware store should have thanked you—not me—for running the cart back into the store.

It's too bad she doesn't know you. But she's seen your work.

✢ ✢ ✢

153

44

Give the Gift of Yourself
This Season

The young boy and his father walked through the snow-covered streets of the city, pushing against the press of Christmas shoppers. They were hunting. Hunting for a Christmas present for the boy. As they walked the streets surveying the goods of the pushcart peddlers, the boy's eyes were drawn to shiny expensive things while the father, who had little money, had something less costly in mind. Each time the boy found something he wanted, his father shook his head no—it was too expensive. And each time the father found something he could afford the boy was not interested. They had worked the entire street without success. Now they found themselves at the end of the street without a present. Years later, the boy would recall the scene:

I heard my father jingle some coins in his pocket. In a flash I knew it all. He'd gotten together about seventy-five cents to buy me a Christmas present and he hadn't dared say so in case there was nothing to be had for so small a sum. As I looked up at him I saw a look of despair and disappointment in his eyes that brought me closer to him than I had ever been in my life.

I wanted to throw my arms around him and say, "It doesn't matter...I understand...This is better than a shiny toy...I love you." But instead we stood shivering beside each other for a long moment—then turned away from the last two pushcarts and started silently back

*home. I didn't even take his hand on the way home
nor did he take mine. We were not on that basis. Nor
did I ever tell him how close to him I felt that night—
that for a little while the concrete wall between father
and son had crumbled away and I knew that we were
two lonely people struggling to reach each other.*

The saddest words in the English language are "if only."
You hear them being said everyday across our city, state and
nation. "If only I had spent more time with my children
while they were young." "If only we had played together
more and watched TV less." "If only I hadn't spent all my
time and energy at the job." If only.

The words "if only" would make a sad, but fitting motto for
many of us today. We live in an age of multiple demands
and pressures, bills to pay, deadlines to meet, customers to
satisfy and Internets to surf. Some say it's harder to be a kid
now than it was in the past, and that is no doubt true. But
it's also harder to be a parent—at least an effective parent
that invests both quality and quantity time with their children. A parent who takes the time to both play and discipline, to encourage and correct, to laugh and to cry with
these little people we call children. It takes both quality
and quantity time to break the "concrete walls" between
parent and child and to reach out and take their hand.

In the midst of raising my own children, I've come to the
conclusion that parents have a choice between being diligent or detached. A diligent parent is a tough thing to be.
A detached parent is infinitely easier. When you're a detached parent you can be present in the home without really "being there." You can go through the motions, pre-

tend to hear what's being said, nod at appropriate times from behind a newspaper or while paying bills, and grunt something unintelligible when a response is required. You don't have to make tough choices about putting family before career, taking the time to read to your children or put aside your work demands to spend Saturday with your little ones. In later years the detached parent doesn't have to worry about imposing curfews, bird-dogging report cards, or monitoring friendships. It's enough (so the detached parent thinks) that they provide a home and meals. That's as much as they received from their parents.

To be a diligent parent requires walking a more difficult path. It's a passage strewn with inconveniences and frustrations. It calls for a sacrifice of time and a reservation of energy at the end of the day. It calls for the extra effort to go to that open house at school, check to see if homework is done, watch the friendships that are forming and—the least popular task of all—imposing consequences and discipline when appropriate. In short, being a diligent parent requires both quality time *and* quantity time. It calls for patience and perseverance. It demands sacrifice of one's own needs and wants in the best interest of the child.

This kind of sacrifice isn't popular. In an era of satisfying our own desires and "self-actualization," the thought of parental sacrifice is about as popular as a New York Yankee fan in Atlanta's Fulton County Stadium. But then sacrifice has never been fashionable or chic. It's routinely dull and tiresome. It doesn't catch national headlines and hardly ever wins awards. But the reward of sacrifice is not found in the moment, or even the year of the sacrifice. It's most often found down the road, perhaps a generation removed. What a father says to his children may not be listened to by the world, but it will be heard loud and clear by his grandchildren.

A parent's sacrifice of time is the true test of genuine devotion and, perhaps, the only way children really know we care. Reach out to your children today, regardless of their age. Touch them. Hold them. Tell them you care. Especially as you Christmas shop with them this season, don't let an opportunity to reach out to them slip away. Chip away at those "concrete walls" and hold your child's hand. Give your family the gift of yourself this season.

45

Helping Older Parents Leads to Good Return

As I walked into the hospital room I saw his familiar face peeking out above white bed sheets, his snowy hair blending into the pillow. Tired eye lids fluttered open at the sound of my feet and through a weak smile my dad said, "I'm glad you're here, Jim." My father, now 76 years old, had suffered a stroke while driving. Neither the car accident nor the stroke was life threatening to dad, but I certainly felt threatened.

Someone once told me that we face our own mortality when our parents die; I was just beginning to understand that saying. My dad, a man who had never been in a hospital before and who always seemed so strong, was now weak and in need of help. It was a first for both of us.

I traveled to Syracuse to be with Dad for a time of role reversal. After release from the hospital we took him home, and I helped feed him, just as he used to feed me. I read to him, just as he used to read to me. I held his hand and took him on unsteady walks over the uneven sidewalks of our neighborhood, just as he used to do with me. I reminded him that, "This too shall pass," just as he used to say to me. ("Where'd you get that dumb saying?" he asked me.) I prayed for him, sat for hours with him and hurt for him—all things he used to do with me when I was a child.

My dad needed me then as much as I had needed him years

before, and I didn't consider it a burden or an inconvenience to do whatever I could to help—just as he never felt that way when I needed him. I don't know, maybe he did feel like it was a burden sometimes, but if he did he never said anything about it. He just stayed by my side to support, to guide, to assist and to push me to do things for myself whenever I could. Now I had to do some of those same things for him.

When we are young and strong it's easy to forget we were once weak and dependent. It is also easy to forget we will, most likely, be weak and dependent again. When we're young and strong we rush impatiently through life, often brushing past people who need our smile, our touch, our encouragement. Someone who needs ten minutes and a listening ear. We hurry by the elderly person who looks a bit confused in the grocery store and never stop to see if we can help. We shuffle our feet impatiently behind an older gentleman counting change at the check-out stand and sigh our frustration aloud. We honk our car horn the nano-second the traffic light turns green if the white-haired lady in front of us doesn't put the pedal to the metal. In short, we fail to slow down long enough to show kindness to those who move slower, talk slower and live slower. These golden aged ones were once beset with the stresses of work and family as we now are. Perhaps they are the ones who changed your diaper, took you for walks, spooned food into your mouth and allowed you to be dependent on them. But now their lives are quite different.

Family life has always meant interdependence. It's where we say in word and deed, "I'll take care of you when you hurt and you'll take care of me when I hurt." The wise king

Solomon said in the Old Testament book of Ecclesiastes, "Two are better than one for they have a good return for their labor, for when one falls down the other can pick him up." Your parents have probably picked you up many times. They gave of themselves—mostly without complaint—when you needed them. As they grow older be sure to do unto them as they have done unto you—or better. Take time to listen to the stories you've heard a hundred times before (they listened to *you* read *your* favorite book a hundred times over). Be patient when they get easily confused over things you readily understand (they took their time trying to explain things to *you* when *you* were young and confused).

Maybe your parents *weren't* there for you as a child, and you're not inclined to be kind to them now. Maybe you didn't get the care and attention you should have, and you don't feel any compulsion to take care of them. It's then you have to summon the strength of your better self. That's when "ought" replaces "want." That's the time to differentiate yourself from those who only do good to those who've done good to them. We are called by a Divine voice to be noble creatures—made in God's image—the One who gave us the example of selfless love and Who graciously reaches out even to those who reject Him. You must act in that image and in response to that call even if your parents don't "deserve" it.

There's a point in life when the child becomes parent to the parent. Assume that responsibility with the knowledge that you're paying back on an investment someone made in you. Pull alongside an older family member and be reminded of the Solomon's words of wisdom, "two are better than one." When you do, you'll have a good return for your labor.✝

Dads

≈family talk

46

The Importance of
Being There

Many years ago Peter Sellers starred in a movie entitled "Being There." The movie wasn't all that memorable, but it got me thinking about the importance of really "being there" for your family. Not just in a "call me if you need me" sort of way, but in an "even if you don't call me I'll show up and hang around just in case you do need me" way. My mom and dad were those kind of people, and I wrote a letter to Dad several years ago thanking him for "being there."

Dear Dad,

I was talking to the kids at the supper table tonight about one of my summer jobs during college. Remember when I worked at the unairconditioned auto parts warehouse? Whew! What a dirty, hot, sweaty and looooong summer that was! I recall the pay was pretty good but the days were long, the work was hard and there was no way to get to the warehouse by bus. I didn't own a car back then and you left too early for your job to drop me off in the morning. The only alternative was for me to ride my bike to and from work. If I remember right my job went from 8:30 to 5:30 and I'd get up extra early so I'd have time to get to work, pedaling all the way in the cool of the morning. It wasn't a bad ride in the early hours of the day.

But the ride home was something else. By the time 5:30 rolled around I was beat from a day of unaccustomed hard work. It was hot and during those first days on the job I'd get out of the warehouse, climb on my bike and trudge the long road home. Seems the hills were especially steep on the way home and when I arrived I was hotter, tireder and grumpier than ever. I couldn't even talk in a civil tone to anyone until after I hit the shower.

*One night after a week or so of that routine I stumbled out of the warehouse at 5:30 to discover my bike was gone. Stolen!..or so I thought. Then I heard the familiar horn toot of our family's Chevy and looked across the parking lot to see you sitting there, my bike sticking out of the trunk, tied down with a strap, and you motioning to me to get in. "I thought you could use a ride home," I think you said. Truer words were never spoken. And every night after you got home from **your** hard day of work you'd go home, grab a bite to eat and then head down to pick me up so I wouldn't have to drag myself home up the hills to Hillsdale Avenue. Did I ever tell you how much I appreciated you doing that all those nights? Probably not.*

So tonight at the supper table my kids learned about a hard job their dad once had. But mostly they heard about another dad who was there when he was needed. Someone who said, by his words and his actions, "I'll be there if you need me." Thanks for being there, Dad. Not just in the warehouse parking lot, but all through the years.

You may not be able to give your kids a lot of money, or buy them fancy clothes, or get them a new car for their 16th birthday. But each of us has the ability to "be there." Being there for your family doesn't mean just a physical presence—a snoozing body in front of the television. It means being an active, listening, reaching-out kind of person. Take the initiative with your family. Think of some way you could lighten someone's burden—then act on it—without being asked. Children can do this for parents, parents for kids, spouses for each other. Make this the year you begin to really "be there" for your family!

✛ ✛ ✛

47

Small Sacrifices

It wasn't the worst thing in the world that could happen to a 9-year-old boy, but it seemed pretty devastating at the time. I had taken my son Spence to get a haircut, and our (former) barber had gotten carried away and taken way too much hair off. It was more than a brush cut. I'd seen military personnel with more hair. Spence's head looked like all it needed was some good buffing to bring it to a high gloss. He was, in a word, bald.

The hairstylist had apparently been exasperated by our efforts to get just the right kind of cut and, in a fit of frustration, simply buzzed Spence's head. I was shocked. Spence was mortified. As we made our way home he was as glum and dragged down as I'd ever seen him. It just about killed me to watch his sad little face peer into the bathroom mirror over and over again in horror.

As I tucked him into bed that night and tried to comfort him an idea hit me. "Spence," I said, "let's see how you feel tomorrow morning. If you're still feeling really bad about your haircut I'll go get mine cut the same way and at least we can be twins until the hair grows back in." He studied my face to see if I was serious. I was. "Thanks a lot, Daddy. Ok. I'll let you know in the morning."

As I walked out of the room, gently closing the door behind me, I tried to visualize what I'd look like with no hair. A buzzed lawyer—going into court—trying to get the jury to take me seriously but looking like a recent escapee from Virginia Military Institute. It wouldn't be a pretty sight. Then I thought about someone who had made a similar kind of sacrifice for me years ago.

I was 18 when I was diagnosed with diabetes. It came as quite a shock to everyone in my family. We knew that Grandpa had a little touch of "sugar," but we didn't know much else about the disease. When the doctors told me I'd have to swear off sugar, my dad decided he would too. Just so I'd have a companion on this new sugar-less journey he said. "I want to know what you're going through," Pa said. "If you can give up sugar, I can too." And from that day forward he didn't use sugar. My dad still doesn't take sugar in his coffee, twenty-five years later, because he made a promise to share in my limitation. Although I know my dad made numerous, more substantial sacrifices for me over the years, none spoke more eloquently or profoundly to me than his sacrifice of sugar.

Back in the modern-era Priest family, I was relieved when Spence woke up the next morning and decided his haircut wasn't as awful as he thought the night before. "That's OK Daddy, you don't have to get your hair cut, but thanks anyway." I have to admit I was greatly relieved. But I would have willingly sacrificed my hair for a few weeks because of the example I had of a man willing to sacrifice sugar for 25 years.

Parents have made sacrifices through the ages for their children. Some folks work long hours to make enough money to send their kids to college. Others give up an overly demanding career in order to spend necessary time with their

family. But it's the little, everyday sacrifices that are sometimes the most memorable. It's those sacrifices when we
identify with the pain or the grief or the sacrifice that our
children are going through that speak most directly to their
hearts. It's like the admonition in the New Testament book
of Romans that says we should "weep with those who weep
and rejoice with those who rejoice." When our children see
us sharing in some way in their sacrifices—when they see us
identifying with them and trying to fully understand the
difficulties they're going through—that's when heart con-
nects to heart. That's when life is knit to life. That's when
an example is laid down worth imitating.

Keep your eyes open for small sacrifices you can make for
your children in the every day events of life. A little sacrifice of sugar can make life sweeter.

48

Say Thanks on Father's Day

Bill Havens was a young man with great athletic talent. In the summer of 1924 he was selected to represent the United States at the Olympics in Paris. His event: canoeing. And Havens was predicted to bring home the gold.

Only problem was, Havens' wife was due to give birth during the same time as the Olympic games, and Havens was faced with the decision of a lifetime. He could head off for Paris and compete in the Olympics or remain behind and be present for the birth of his first child. The gold medal in canoeing or the gold medal in fathering. He made the decision to stay home, and his fellow Americans left for Paris without him. On August 1, 1924, his son Frank was born— four days *after* the Games.

Did Havens make the right choice? He thought so. Especially when he received a telegram, years later, in the summer of 1952 from Helsinki where the summer Olympics were being held. The telegram read: "Dear Dad…Thanks for waiting around for me to get born in 1924. I'm coming home with the gold medal you should have won. Your loving son, Frank." Frank Havens, Bill's son, won the gold medal in the same Olympic canoeing event his dad was going to compete in 18 years earlier.

Which of the Havens' men won the gold medal? I'd say both of them. Frank won the canoeing event, but Bill won the gold in fatherhood. And, importantly, Frank remembered to say thanks to his dad—something we can do this Father's Day.

It's a sad but true fact that the number of long distance phone calls on Father's Day is only a fraction of the number made on Mother's Day. More of us call Mom to remember her in May than call Dad in June. Why is that? Perhaps Mom was around more in our growing up years. Maybe we feel more comfortable talking to her. Or could it be that Dad simply went about doing his job in a quiet way that we didn't always notice? Whatever the reason, this sorry statistic needs to be changed. We need to make more long distance calls to Dad on Father's Day.

But what would we say during our call? How about these suggestions as a starting place?

– "Thanks for serving in the military, Dad, and defending our nation's freedom."

– "I appreciate your faithfulness in going to work each day to provide for our family, Daddy."

– "Father, thanks for teaching me about cars (or checking accounts, or lawn-mowing or whatever else he taught you)."

–"Daddy, thanks for being a model of a what a man should be."

– "Pop, thanks for disciplining me over the years—even though I didn't like it very much at the time!"

– "Pa, thanks for taking me to a house of worship each

week and teaching me about God."

I know many folks may not have good memories of their father; still others may have no memory at all. Some of our dads were not good examples or were absent or were uninvolved in our lives. But along the way, somewhere, in some way, your dad probably did something right. He made some sacrifice for you at some point. He put your interests ahead of his own at least once. Scan your memory banks carefully to find at least one thing to thank your dad for and give him a call this Father's Day.

Bill Havens treasured his son's telegram more than he would have treasured an Olympic gold medal. Your dad will treasure your phone call the same way.

✝ ✝ ✝

49

Joseph, the Forgotten Father

He was not an absentee dad, although he could have easily turned out that way. His fiancee was pregnant with a child he knew was not his. He could have been angry. He could have been hurt. He could have taken the easy way and just dumped her. But he chose to take a more difficult road. He stuck by the woman and offered his name to both her and the unborn child. Was he crazy—or divinely inspired?

Joseph, the earthly parent of Jesus of Nazareth, is a person who doesn't get much favorable publicity. This unheralded dad of Christmas past could use a better press agent. In all the Christmas plays put on by churches around the country this season, some little guy will get the part of Joseph. He'll stand silently by the manger in a bathrobe and shuffle his feet. He won't have any lines to speak. He won't even get to hold the plastic baby Jesus. The Joseph of our Christmas pageants is the silent type.

The Christmas songs we sing this season will scarcely make mention of this father figure. As far as we know Joseph was a virgin, just like Mary, but how many choirs will sing, "Round yon virgin, *father* and child"? Can you imagine hearing, "What child is this who's laid to rest on *Joseph's* lap is sleeping"? No, there won't be a tune sung for Joseph this Christmas.

We'd have to admit, of all the Christmas characters, Joseph

sits in the back row—mostly left out—playing second fiddle. But there are some strong character traits of this man from Nazareth that serve as a good example to fathers of the current generation.

‑ First, Scripture tells us that Joseph was a "just" man. When his bride-to-be turned up pregnant he would have had the right, under the laws of the time, to have her stoned. This unexpected pregnancy that he was not responsible for was probably a source of embarrassment for him. But he put honor before pride and took his fiancee's feelings into consideration. He decided he would not disgrace Mary. *Joseph was a family man who put others first.*

‑ We also see Joseph did not act rashly or hastily. The Bible says, "While he *considered* these things an angel of the Lord appeared to him saying, 'Do not be afraid to take Mary as your wife'" (Matthew 1:20). Joseph took time to consider his actions. The knee-jerk reaction of most men of his day would have been to put an end to the murmurs and rumors quickly. Instead, Joseph weighed his options carefully before he took action. *Joseph was a family man who was thoughtful, not reactive, in his deeds.*

‑ Joseph was man of obedience to God's will. The world's common sense told him to do one thing, but the sovereign God of the universe told him something different. Joseph listened to God instead of the world. He didn't waver. He didn't wait. The Scripture says, "And Joseph arose from his sleep and did as the angel of the Lord commanded him." *Joseph was a family man who obeyed God without debate or delay.*

— And Joseph hung in there for the long term. It would have been easy for Joseph to be disillusioned with the back-stage role he played. He might have been frustrated with all the attention given to Mary and the Christ child. But instead, Joseph recognized he had a specific mission. Like the special-teams' player in football or the pinch hitter in baseball, Joseph didn't whine about not having center stage all to himself. Instead, he hung in there and helped raise the boy Jesus to manhood. Joseph's contribution as a father is well reflected in the commentary of Jesus' growth to manhood. "And Jesus grew in wisdom and stature and in favor with God and man" (Luke 2:52). If it's true that the acorn doesn't fall far from the tree, Joseph stands like a mighty, if quiet, oak in the life of Christ. *Joseph was a family man who made a life-long commitment and stuck with it.*

In a time when absentee fathers seem to abound, when dads sometimes neglect or abandon their children and wives, when men are searching for a genuine example of authentic fatherhood, we need look no farther than the man from Nazareth. If we could vote for "Father of the ages," I'd have to throw my vote to Joseph. You see, I'm pro-Joe. Maybe you should be too. In all the hurry and flurry of Christmas shopping, gift wrapping and sounds of the season, we would do well to look to Joseph as a model for fatherhood.

50

Boy Training

A New York banker was talking to one of his rich, Texas clients on the phone when the Texan invited the Yankee to come visit him. "Why don't I send my jet up to New York this weekend to pick up you and your wife, and you can join us at our son's ranch outside Austin?" said the Texan. "The boy's got 100,000 acres of land stocked with horses and cattle and a beautiful house with a huge swimming pool. Yep, I'm real proud of the boy because he earned it all by himself." The banker was impressed and said, "Sounds like your son has done very well for himself. How old is he?" "He's eight," said the Texan. "Eight?!" shouted the banker. "How could he earn enough money to buy all that?" "He got four A's and one B," replied the Texan.

This dad had invested heavily in his son. Unfortunately, we don't know if he invested the right way with the boy. Dads who invest only money in their children soon learn the return on investment is not very great. The better investment is to spend your time and energy—not your money—on your boy.

I've found that men investing in boys has been a topic of conversation for many, many years. While picking curiously through an antique shop last year I ran across a little book that caught my eye. Printed in 1912, it was entitled *Boy Training* and was a compilation of essays by various authorities at the time, all who had an opinion about the proper way to raise a boy. Since I am in the midst of trying to grow one of those creatures myself, I thought I could use some help from these wise men of old so I purchased the volume. It turned out to be one of my better purchases at an antique store.

I doubt the book has much value as an "antique," but it has been very valuable in other ways. It reminded me about how important it is for grown men to be actively involved in the lives of growing young men. As John Alexander, then Secretary of the Boy Scouts of America said in his Introduction to that 1912 book: "There is no *boy* problem (in America), it is a *man* problem." It's still true today.

Everyone is concerned about crime today, and one of the sad facts to be faced is that most crime is committed by young men or young boys. We can continue to stew and fret over building more jails, adding more correction staff and revoking the early release program, or we can attack the problem at its root. Young men need male role models who will give discipline and encouragement.

If all young men had a father or father figure to give them moral guidance would that mean the end of crime? Probably not. But would it put a big dent in the crime statistics? You bet it would.

So here's a plea for men to take an active role in the lives of boys. If you're living at home with your son, make a conscious decision to make a difference in his life. Spend time with him. Take him with you when you run errands or work on chores. Coach his team (but don't put too much pressure on him *please!*). Simply spending time with him is a great way to build a relationship foundation with your son. Your conversations during these times don't have to be deep, but you'll find you can talk about important issues a lot more easily with your heads over an automobile engine than you can sitting face-to-face across a table. Relationships are built a little at a time.

Relationship building is critical for single dads too. If you're divorced and separated from your son, stay in contact with him by phone and by letter. Spend time with him in person as often as you can. Let him know you're proud to have him as a son, even though you can't be there all the time. Begin to establish yourself as a presence in his world. If you haven't been close in the past, don't expect an overnight miracle. Gentle persistence is the key here. If he gets the idea you're sincere and you continue to be faithful at building that relationship, chances are he'll eventually open up.

One good thing I've learned about being a dad is that you don't need to have all the right answers. It's all right for your son to hear you say, "I don't know," and it's fine for him to see you cry. Break down the barriers and get involved before your boy becomes a man. True, all this takes time and energy, and if you add this responsibility to your already full plate of duties, it may feel a little overwhelming. But once you get started you'll find it's not as difficult as you think. It's like putting money in the bank. At the beginning it seems hard to save, but if you make regular deposits in your account you'll soon have a growing nest egg. The same principle applies to boys. A regular investment of time and interest will reap rewards in a lasting, loving relationship. That's a return on investment that yields great dividends!

And some men can go an extra step and spend a little time with a boy who doesn't have a dad at all. There are lots of single moms out there who would welcome someone to spend time with their sons. Perhaps it could be through scouting, or coaching sports or teaching in your synagogue or church. Keep your eyes open for a young man upon whom you could make an impact in some small way. You can make a difference in a boy's life by simply deciding to be involved and letting him know you care.

Spending time with a boy is an investment worth far more than a Texas ranch. It's an investment in the future—yours, the boy's and the world's.

51

Dads Can Help Daughters Become Competent Women

In his book, *Always Daddy's Girl*, Norm Wright tells about a grown woman named Victoria and her relationship with her dad:

> *My memories of my father are unpleasant and vague. He didn't seem that interested in me at any time when I was growing up. He was brusque and gruff. One of the things I hated most was his anger. He would shout and storm around and then not talk to any of us for several days. For some reason I always felt responsible for his outbursts. And Dad practically lived at work. It was like pulling teeth to get him to take a vacation. I guess I hoped for so much more from him. A word of praise here, a compliment there. He just grunted when I showed him my high school prom dress. When I call him now on the phone we talk a little but it's never anything more than surface level. I wish he would open up to me. He talks for awhile and then says "Here's your mother."*

For good or ill, a father has a tremendous impact on his daughter. *From* him she first learns about men—how they act, what they like, how they treat women. *With* him she learns about herself: Is she competent? Is she pretty? Does this man like her for what she is? *Without* him she languishes: Why has he rejected me? Did he ever love me? Was I not good enough? Whether he is absent or present, harsh or gentle, withdrawn or open, a girl learns much from her dad. And how he treats her—or doesn't—will dramatically affect her the rest of her life.

How can a dad help a young girl grow into a competent woman?

Begin early. Right from the cradle every dad should take the initiative to be involved in his daughter's life. Don't let your wife edge you out, even unintentionally, from an active role with your little girl. Participate in dressing her, fixing her hair (give it your best shot!), and taking her with you when you go out. Read to her and sing to her (even if you can't carry a tune). The process of winning her heart begins early —so spend as much time as possible with your little one. Assert yourself gently as a presence in her life.

Assist her in becoming a competent person. When your daughter is still young, teach her the same things you would teach a son. Show her how to play catch and change a tire. Reveal to her the world of tools. Never (repeat—NEVER!) tell her it's not her place to try something non-traditional, a task or an activity usually reserved for boys. Do whatever you can to pass along the same life skills you would teach your son.

Be high touch. Despite the fact that sexual harassment and sexual abuse are daily front page news, dads must be "high touch" with both their sons and their daughters. Usually this isn't a problem with little girls—cuddly little things who are easy to hug and kiss. The problem comes when they reach puberty. As a daughter begins developing into a woman (usually between ages 11 to 14), many dads feel awkward and uncomfortable about hugging and withdraw physical affection from their daughters at a time the girls need it most. This is the age young women begin asking, "Am I pretty?" "Am I loved?" "Am I accepted?" A withdrawing dad can, unintentionally, send a negative answer to these questions when he withdraws physical affection. Fathers must fight through that feeling of discomfort and stay in physical touch with their daughters or the young woman may end up looking for that missing affection in the arms of another male.

Speak words of love and honor. Most men, by nature or training, don't do a great job verbally communicating their feelings. This is especially true with daughters. Like Victoria in the Norm Wright story, we often withhold our verbal approval to our daughters. Don't make the mistake of silence. Speak to your girl. Tell her you love her, that she's valuable and that you like the woman she's becoming. Break down the wall between daddy and daughter with well-timed words.

Keep at it. Sometimes the best intentioned dads are kept at arm's length by their daughters. Some days (or weeks or months) dads just aren't "cool" with their girls, especially in the teen years. When this happens don't give into the temptation to chuck the whole relationship. Gentle persistence is the key to your daughter's heart. When you get the "rolling eyes," the dramatic sighs, the banging bedroom doors or the outburst of emotions, don't take it personally. These things are the ebb and flow of life in a young woman. Ride the emotional waves just as you would ride the waves of a lake when you're out in a boat fishing. When the boat rocks back and forth, you don't bail out or head for shore—you just hang on tight and keep fishing. Do the same thing with your daughter, and you will eventually bring in your catch.

Dads are a critically important part of their daughter's life. Do all you can to insure that your girl grows up to be a happy and competent young woman.

52

Listen Carefully to the Ones You Love

I recently wrote my dad a letter that brought back a lot of memories for both of us. And it reminded me about the importance of listening carefully to the ones you love. After checking with local Postal Service authorities I have determined it is lawful for you to intercept and read this piece of mail:

Dear Dad,

I saw you sitting at my supper table tonight, Dad. Of course you weren't really there. You were at your fishing camp on Tuscarora Lake, not in Oklahoma City, but you were there nonetheless. After finishing supper Spence was talking with me about his day and I found myself sitting with both elbows on the table, hands together, fingers interlaced, head cocked to one side, listening and nodding as he talked. Then I remembered where I had seen that scene before. It was about 30 years ago around a kitchen table in Syracuse, New York. Another brown-haired, 11-year-old boy was excitedly telling his dad all about his day—and his dad pushed an empty supper plate aside, put his elbows on the table, hands together, fingers interlaced, head cocked to one side, nodding his head, listening intently. It was you listening to me. You always told me I could tell you anything and even though I didn't always tell you everything, it wasn't because you weren't there and will-

ing to listen.

You know, I don't remember that we had too many formal "talks." You seldom, if ever, sat me down for a lecture or said, "Let me set you straight about this, son." A lot of the time we spent together was marked by silence. Sometimes we were riding in a car, sometimes sitting in the woods waiting for deer to appear, sometimes working on some broken appliance, sometimes sitting on a smooth-as-glass lake in the early morning, as the bass hit flies on the surface. The silence would be broken occasionally by some observation you'd make, or by a question I'd ask, then it would be quiet again. But the silence wasn't the awkward kind that you feel when you've just met someone and don't know what to say. It was a comfortable silence—like a well-worn moccasin or an old sweater that's been broken in—it felt natural. I guess we both knew if there was something that needed to be said it would come out eventually. We didn't worry about the quiet spots in our conversations.

But when we talked I always felt like you really listened. You didn't always agree with me and sometimes I (quietly) disagreed with you, but there was a connection in those conversations that was more than word to ear—it was heart to heart. Remember the time when I was in high school and you said you weren't going to vote in the election because you thought both candidates were worthless? I told you if you didn't vote you were giving up on America and you had to go vote. You ended up reconsidering and voted and I remember thinking to myself—"He really listened to what I had to say."

And remember when I came home from college, heart sick over some girl who had jilted me? As we painted the house that evening you asked me, "Want a little advice about women?" "Not really, Dad," I said. I figured I knew what you were going to say—the old "there are other fish in the sea" talk. I could see by the look in your eyes you were hurt, but you didn't say anything and you didn't offer any advice. A few days later, when I came back to ask you what your advice was on the subject, you didn't even act smug. You just picked up where we left off and you gave me the old "there are other fish in the sea" talk. It's true—I had heard the talk before but I knew you cared. And you listened to my hurt. (You know, Dad, you were right about the fish!)

I guess what I'm trying to say is thanks for listening. To all my silly jabbering as a kid, to my stories of love lost as a teenager, to my struggles as a father—you still haven't given up listening to me. I hope I'm passing on that legacy to my children by sitting with my elbows on the table, hands together, fingers interlaced, listening intently and nodding while they talk to me.

Gotta go put the kids to bed—and listen to their prayers. Talk to you soon.

Much love, Jim

In a world where we are bombarded with information, we sometimes forget to really listen to what our family members are saying to us. When we get home after work we're tired and ready to relax. Listening—*real listening*—is hard work, and we are sometimes too tired or too busy to pay close attention to the conversation in our homes. True listening requires us to hear both the words and what's *behind* the words spoken by those we love. It takes patience and undivided attention, but it's worth the effort because we're building a relationship with someone who will really listen to *us* when we need it.

The good Lord gave us two ears and one mouth. We should use them in that proportion. Listen carefully to the words spoken by those you love.

53

I Like to Be
Chosen

Author Bob Benson told a story that sounded like a page out of my own life. Bob said he was a scrawny little kid and was always the last guy picked when teams chose sides for a playground baseball game. After the team captains had chosen all their friends as well as the good hitters and good fielders, the teacher would say, "You can't play until one team takes Bob." One of the captains would stare downward, dig his toe in the ground, and reluctantly say, "Oh all right, we'll take him." Bob played "pigtail" behind the right fielder in deep, deep right field. You don't get many balls hit to deep right field in elementary school. Bob claimed he never even got up to bat until the 5th grade. So Bob said it was especially meaningful to him when he read John 15:16 in the New Testament. Jesus said, "You did not choose Me, but I chose you and appointed you to bear much fruit." Bob used to say, "I like that because I like to be chosen."

I like to be chosen too. I wasn't little and scrawny like Bob when I was a kid. I was pudgy and slow. I was always one of the last kids to be selected for the teams too. So it was especially meaningful to me to hear the story of how my dad chose to place me—and our family—as a priority in his life.

I grew up in a home where labor unions were important. My great grandfather died in the coal mines of Pennsylvania before there were unions. He was killed during a cave-in one morning, but the company wouldn't stop work to take him to the surface. He laid in the bottom of the mine all day until the end of the shift. Then he was taken home in a wheelbarrow and dumped on the back porch. No worker's compensation. No insurance. My grandfather, who was twelve years old at the time, took his place the next day. He had to. The family lived in a company owned house and owed money to the company store. It's little wonder that my grandfather joined a labor union as soon as one was formed. My dad did too. Union blood ran hot and deep in my family.

When I was born in 1955 my father had been elected president of his local labor union. He was gone a lot on trips, and the schedule was demanding. Dad was a good speaker and a smart man. He was good looking and a good organizer. The national union wanted to move him up. His responsibilities in the union increasingly took him away from home. His family responsibilities received less and less of his time. Mom could see a storm brewing. One night she sat down and had a talk with dad. "You have a daughter and a son, and they're starting to grow up without you. You have to make a choice: you can spend all your time with the union, or you can spend time with your family."

Years later, as I heard this story retold, I wondered what thoughts ran through my dad's mind. He could have had a rewarding career. He might even have been famous. Surely he would have helped many people. But he chose his family instead. He chose me. And it's a choice that has always made me feel valuable and loved. Loved by my mother for talking to Dad. Loved by my father for giving up something important so I could have a daily dad.

Careers and work are important. They put food on our tables and give our lives meaning and purpose. But our jobs should never be the source of our self worth. That must come from our relationship with God. He has chosen us and appointed us to bear fruit.

Our jobs should never become more important than marriage and family. We have to make a choice, as my dad did, to place a priority on family. It may mean giving up an alluring promotion. It might require us to cut back our hours on the job. It will undoubtedly mean making little decisions every day to leave our work at work and to really be home when we're home.

We all have to make choices. Sometimes small. Sometimes significant. It's my prayer that you will choose to place a priority on your marriage and family. It's what my dad did decades ago when he chose me. I will be forever grateful for his choice, because–I like to be chosen.